JACKIE ROBINSON

JACKIE ROBINSON
Between the Baselines

By Glenn Stout and Dick Johnson

With Essays By
David Halberstam
Red Smith
Wendell Smith
Gerald Early
Ira Berkow
Luke Salisbury

Woodford Press
San Francisco

Glenn Stout is a freelance writer and editor. A graduate of Bard College, he is the author for the text for, *Ted Williams, A Portrait in Words and Pictures*, and *Joe DiMaggio: An Illustrated Life*. He also serves as series editor for the annual anthology *The Best American SportsWriting*. He is a frequent contributor to a number of national publications and is a columnist for *Boston Baseball*. A native of Amlin, Ohio, he lives in Uxbridge, Massachusetts.

Dick Johnson serves as curator of The Sports Museum of New England in Cambridge, Massachusetts. He has previously edited and co-authored five books, including *Ted Williams, A Portrait in Words and Pictures*, *Joe DiMaggio: An Illustrated Life, Young at Heart, The Story of Johnny Kelly, (with Frederick Lewis), The Treasury of Baseball* and *The Twentieth Century Baseball Chronicle*. He is a frequent contributor to national publications and is a member of the Society for American Baseball Research and The Society of Football U.K. (soccer) Statisticians. He is a native of Worcester, Massachusetts, a graduate of Bates College and lives with his family in Milton, Massachusetts.

Published by
WOODFORD PRESS
660 Market Street, Suite 206
San Francisco, California 94104

Creative Director: Laurence J. Hyman
Editor: Rob Kelly
Designer: Jim Santore
Vice President, Marketing & Development: David Lilienstein
Assistant Editor: Wendy Gardner

ISBN: 0-942627-49-0
Library of Congress Card Catalog Number: 96-061809
First Printing: April 1997
Printed and bound in the United States of America
Distributed to the trade by National Book Network

Contents

To the members of the Black Sporting Press, my father, and daughter Saorla.
Glenn Stout

To my girls Mary, Elizabeth, & Minna and my slugger Bobby. And in memory of Natalie Bluthardt.

To the memory of Mabrey "Doc" Kountze, Sports Editor of The Boston Chronicle *and* The Guardian *and the first African-American sportwriter to gain a credential to Fenway Park. He was a pioneer in his profession and a kind and generous friend to Glenn and myself.*
Dick Johnson

Acknowledgments

Thanks to my partner Dick Johnson for his dedication, generosity and enthusiasm. Likewise to my wife Siobhan for her patience and support. I am grateful to the following for their assistance with this volume: the staff of the Lamont Library at Harvard University; the Microtext Department of the Boston Public Library; the Thayer Library in Uxbridge, Massachusetts; the UCLA Sports Information Department; Dan Friedell; Sally Landover; Ken Hartnett; John Dorsey; my teammates on the Braintree Athletics; and Douglas Pikes of the Men's Senior Baseball League. Special thanks to those members of the Brooklyn Dodgers whose insights helped shape this book, namely Gene Hermanski, Ed Stevens and Howie Schultz.
Glenn Stout

My thanks to Glenn Stout for once again plumbing the depths of an American legend and unearthing many hitherto significant, yet obscure details of a life whose truths are far more compelling than the many universally accepted myths that have surrounded it. Glenn's depth of research and clarity of expression should make his text the definitive work of Robinson the ballplayer.

I am greatly indebted to my wife Mary, son Robert and daughter Elizabeth for putting up with the many hours in which daddy couldn't play or mow the lawn. I am also grateful to my colleagues at The Sports Museum of New England for their encouragement and support. In particular I appreciate the help of the following individuals who lightened my editorial load: Mark Torpey, Sports Editor of *The Boston Herald;* John Cronin, librarian extraordinaire of *The Boston Herald;* the ever cheerful Pat Kelly at The National Baseball Library; and to the resourceful Mark Rucker of Transcendental Graphics. Coming through in the clutch with names and numbers were Mary McGrath and Christopher Lydon of WBUR-Boston and John Taylor "Ike" Williams of the Palmer and Dodger Literary Agency.

I appreciate the work of our essayists, especially that of David Halberstam, Gerald Earley and old friend Luke Salisbury. All composed superb original essays for this book. Thanks to Ira Berkow for unearthing one of his gems and thanks also to those writers who, because of schedule, could not contribute to this work but fully support its creation. Among those writers are: Julian Bond, Pete Hamill, George Plimpton, Gen. Colin Powell, John Edgar Wideman, Frank Deford and Henry Louis Gates. I appreciate their kind words. In closing I want to thank Laurence Hyman, David Lilienstein and Rob Kelly of Woodford Publishing. They are publishers of wonderful books that do justice to, and lend insight to, those subjects that make life worth living, namely sports and music.
Dick Johnson

INTRODUCTION

"I don't know nothing about no Jackie Robinson."

Ten years ago, that statement was uttered by Vince Coleman, an African-American Major League Baseball player with the St. Louis Cardinals. Now, there are probably even more people—black and white, young and old, male and female—for whom the name Jackie Robinson means virtually nothing.

The occasion of the fiftieth anniversary of the day Jackie Robinson stepped onto a Major League Baseball diamond and broke the twentieth century color line will, temporarily anyway, rectify that ignorance. There will be exhibits, documentaries, books, magazine articles, special "days" at ballparks all around the country, and other sundry events to mark that special occasion. There were similar remembrances in 1972 on the 25th anniversary, and also in 1987 on the 40th anniversary.

It is different now. As more and more of Robinson's contemporaries pass on, knowledge of the full scope of his accomplishments is endangered. Who Jackie Robinson was and what he really did are in danger of being overlooked, or even more tragically, entirely forgotten. A century ago, when bicycling was one of the most popular sports in America, African-American cyclist Major Taylor was one of the best known athletes

in the world. Few have even heard of him today. There is no assurance that Jack Roosevelt Robinson will be remembered one hundred years from now for anything more than the thumbnail description of him as the first African-American in this century to break organized baseball's "color line."

Is this his most significant and important accomplishment? Absolutely. But is that all for which he should be remembered? Absolutely not.

While statements that profess total ignorance of Robinson are disturbing, it is equally unsettling that even though many recognize Robinson as the man who broke the color line, for most that is the extent of their knowledge. The full breadth of his accomplishment has been upstaged by the glare of the spotlight that shines so brightly on that one single day in Robinson's life.

Only by connecting the events of that single day to the balance of Robinson's life can we gain a sense of what that day meant and how it changed America. Robinson had already lived twenty-eight remarkable, eventful years, and racial prejudice did not cease the instant he took the field. The impact of Robinson's signing by the Dodgers was not fully realized until America had the opportunity to see Robinson, the player, in action; not just over the course of a few weeks or a few months, but over the course of his entire career.

Not that the events of April 15, 1947 don't

deserve such attention, but Robinson's baseball career neither began nor ended on that day. By the time he joined the Dodgers, Robinson had played professional baseball, almost nonstop, for two full years. After that date, he went on to play another 1,381 games in his major league career, plus another 38 games in six different World Series. For much of that time he was the best player in the game.

I am too young to have seen Jackie Robinson play baseball. I barely even remember seeing Robinson on television before his death. Before embarking on this project all I knew about Jackie Robinson had come from reading books on both the Dodgers and Robinson.

While the idea of doing a book about Robinson intrigued me, I must admit that I was not particularly enamored by either the player I read about or the circumstances surrounding his admission to the big leagues. While I understood the significance of his accomplishment and appreciated its effect on the game of baseball, I always sensed that these accounts indulged in more hagiography than biography. I was being given only the outlines of a man, the abridged version of his story, a series of high points.

I wanted to learn more.

Many earlier books and articles about Robinson, including his own various ghost-written efforts, do not focus on the specifics of his career as a player. Neither do they look at his career with a critical eye. His life story is usually painted with a broad brush, where anecdotes often take the place of facts. Some accounts, including those that have appeared under Robinson's own name, suffer from factual errors that range from the annoying to the egregious. Others reflect their age and are inadvertently patronizing in tone and outlook. Some so zealously "protect" Robinson as to be virtually useless as historical documents. They deliver us not the story of a man, but a collection of myths.

Most of these accounts tell the same story. They focus on Robinson's relationship with Dodgers President and part-owner Branch Rickey, highlighting Rickey's famous admonition not to fight back, followed by accounts of the taunts and threats directed at Robinson on and off the field, and culminating with Robinson's eventual "unleashing." Branch Rickey is anointed a hero. Robinson is upheld as the effective agent of Rickey's moral sensibility.

There is nothing intentionally wrong or misleading about such accounts, but they are one reason, amongst many others, why it is possible to "know nothing about no Jackie Robinson." For the story they tell is incomplete and simplistic. The role Robinson played in his own drama is diminished. His many accomplishments are relegated to the background.

The larger story of Robinson's life and career in baseball is more complicated and discrete. Robinson's signing by Rickey was not only a singular act of charity by a singularly moral man, but the almost inevitable result of decades of work by literally hundreds and thousands of invisible heroes who made the integration of baseball their cause, and selected Robinson as their savior. The black press chose Robinson, not Branch Rickey. To his credit, Rickey was wise enough to see what had already been made obvious, courageous enough to act upon it, and, just as significantly, smart enough to know that it made sense from a business standpoint.

Yet it was the way Robinson played the game that made it all work. Had he failed as a player we would not be celebrating Jackie Robinson this season, but some other African-American ballplayer in some other year. Even if Robinson had still been the first twentieth century African-American to play Major League Baseball, had he not gone on to have such glorious success, would we celebrate him in the same way we do today? I doubt it. Few realize that in the months after

Rickey signed Jackie Robinson, he also signed African-American pitcher John Wright to a minor league contract, followed closely by Roy Campanella, Roy Partlow and Don Newcombe. For a time, Wright and Robinson were teammates. Yet because Wright failed and Robinson succeeded, few remember Wright today. He became a footnote in a larger story.

Only the most zealous of sports fans today are able to name the first African-Americans in pro football, basketball, or hockey. Why? In part, it is because baseball enjoyed a much higher profile than those other sports in American society at mid-century. But it is also because those other pioneers did not go on to dominate their sport as Robinson did. Had Robinson been only an average player, he might still be remembered today, but he would not be celebrated.

Robinson was better than good. He was a great player. Given the pressures imposed upon him, he was magnificent. When one considers the odd and arduous path he took on his way to the major leagues, his success tests the borders of believability. Consider this: In the spring of 1940, at age 21, Robinson played in fewer than two dozen games for the UCLA varsity baseball team, playing poorly and hitting a paltry .097. The following spring, concluding that his education was virtually worthless, he quit school prior to graduation, not even bothering to stay on another few months to play baseball his senior year. Of the four sports in which he lettered at UCLA, baseball was clearly his least favorite. Over the next four years, from 1941 thru 1944, he worked as a camp counselor, played semi-pro football and basketball, served in the Army, and coached small college basketball. Except for a few brief months at the camp in the spring of 1941, the odd playground game, a one-day tryout with the Chicago White Sox in March of 1942 and some pick-up ball while in the Army in 1944, he did not play baseball.

Yet in 1945, almost on a lark, he tried out for and joined the Kansas City Monarchs of the Negro American League, then the preeminent black team in America. Before he played a game, he vaulted past hundreds of more experienced, more deserving and more talented players, and was invited to try out for the Boston Red Sox. Although the Red Sox passed on signing him, the tryout instantly made him one of the best known players in Negro baseball. And while many of his teammates were unimpressed with his ability, he played 47 games, hit .387, and was selected to play shortstop in the East-West all-star game.

In the winter of 1945, Branch Rickey signed him to a contract with the Dodgers AAA farm club, the Montreal Royals of the International League. He was moved to second base, led the International League in hitting and led the Royals to victory in the Junior World Series. In 1947, he was moved to first base, promoted to the Dodgers and was the best rookie in the major leagues. He was transferred back to second base in 1948, and in 1949 he was named the Most Valuable Player in the National League.

Has any other player, ever, spent so much time away from the game and decided so late in his life to play, then performed so magnificently? Look at the records of Mays, Aaron, Cobb, Williams or DiMaggio. The very best players improve exponentially in their early twenties before peaking at the age of twenty-four or twenty-five. Robinson hardly played during that critical time period. No other major league player has ever taken such a disjointed path, at longer odds, to reach the major leagues, and then, under almost unbelievable pressure, performed so well.

According to the hagiography, Branch Rickey conducted a thorough investigation of Robinson's background. Yet not even he knew what a wonderful choice he had made. Robinson was perhaps the only black player so well equipped to suffer the inevitable agonies of being the first

African-American in Major League Baseball. For Robinson had plenty of experience being the "first" to do just about everything he did in life. And even when he was not, technically, "the first," he was often the first in his situation to realize and see what was happening, and, just as importantly, to try to do something about it.

The Robinson family was no stranger to being trailblazers. When Jackie's mother, Mallie Robinson, took her children from Georgia to California in 1920, the Robinson's unknowingly became pioneers in the migration of American blacks to California. At the time, relatively few African-American families were able to leave the segregation and economic poverty of the South and travel across the country. Later, as one of the few black families in Pasadena, Mallie Robinson overcame the odds and purchased a house. The Robinsons became, literally, the first black family on their street.

Each day when Jackie or his other siblings went to school, the playground, to the movies, or even downtown shopping, they risked becoming the first African-American to do something in Pasadena. At each step, there was the potential of a fight for their civil rights. Even at a young age, Jackie Robinson was acutely aware of the limits he faced solely due to the color of his skin.

Unlike many African-Americans of his generation, Robinson refused to accept the limitations imposed by others. When confronted with racism, he challenged it, learning both the danger and the opportunity such challenges presented.

He learned that any achievement came with a price and that nothing could ever make up for the fact, as Robinson wrote in his own autobiography, "I was a black man in a white world. I never had it made."

There were lessons all around. In 1936, Robinson's brother, Mack Robinson, earned a spot on the U.S. Olympic team and even won a silver medal in the 200-meter run at the 1936

Games in Berlin. But Mack's Olympic experience was rife with racism, not so much that perpetrated by the Nazis, but by his own Olympic team and coaches. Although Olympic success carried no assurance of financial gain, Mack was still embittered by the fact that his medal didn't even win him the right to a good job. Upon returning from Berlin, he went to work as a common laborer.

Later, when Jackie attended Pasadena Junior College and UCLA to play sports, he was one of the first blacks to do so. And these earlier lessons were not lost on him: he never believed that athletic achievement guaranteed equality, or that the cheers of the crowd brought everlasting respect. After quitting UCLA he underwent a similar experience. In the service Robinson banged headlong into the institutionalized racism of the American military. He had to fight for a chance to become an officer, and then, when he asserted his rights on a bus on an army base, he paid the price. He was threatened with a court martial and eventually dismissed from service.

All these events contributed to his character, and all played a part in his development as a ballplayer. Yet that was not enough to guarantee his success.

For while Robinson may have been the player best prepared for the mental challenge of breaking the color line, at the same time, Rickey's choice of Robinson was odd. There were questions about his ability. Stardom was no certainty, and neither was his capacity to fulfill the role that Rickey demanded he play. As a twenty-six-year-old rookie, Robinson was inexperienced and a little old. He could run, but he didn't hit with much power, had a weak arm and was plagued by a chronically bad ankle. His glove was only adequate. Furthermore, he wasn't even close to being the best player in the Negro Leagues.

As a black man, Robinson was considered "uppity" and a potential troublemaker. He had always run up against authority, and when told he could not do something, he tended to react with belligerence.

Branch Rickey was asking Jackie to do something he had shown absolutely no prior propensity to do, he asked Jackie to bury his personal feelings and act for the greater good.

Robinson did, and perhaps that's why he succeeded where he might not have. For on the field, focused and fixed on the task at hand, whether that was stealing second, turning the double play or beating out a bunt, in the midst of playing the game he was able to experience what he otherwise could not, the very principle he was fighting for: freedom.

This volume strives to achieve several purposes. I have tried to provide a thorough account of Robinson's early life, to take a critical look at the circumstances that led him to the major leagues, and to provide a detailed accounting of his career as a player. Original essays and reprints by notable writers have been included to add other voices to this project. Through the photographs selected by Dick Johnson, we hope to capture something of the indefinable essence of the man.

When I first considered this project some four years ago, my goal was to undercover the whys, hows, wheres, and whens of Robinson's remarkable career in baseball. For in the fifty years since he broke into the game, that part of his story has suffered. To say only that "Robinson was the first African-American to break the color line" is as incomplete a description of his vast accomplishments as is his .311 lifetime batting average. Jackie Robinson was more than any one line or one statistic can describe.

It is the author's hope that after reading this book, you will feel confident that you now "know something about Jackie Robinson."

The primary resource materials used in the writing of this biography have been the microfilm edition of newspapers, namely the New York Herald Tribune, The New York Times, the Los Angeles Times, the Louisville Courier Journal, the Montreal Gazette, the Pittsburgh Courier, The Daily Worker, the Boston Chronicle, the Boston Guardian, the Los Angeles Sentinel, The Sporting News and various others. Previous book-length treatments of Robinson provided background and filled in gaps where newspaper accounts were incomplete, as did a number of magazine articles, primarily those listed in Myron Smith's "Baseball Bibliography."

Interviews with a number of former ballplayers and observers played a key role in this project. Conversations with Ed Stevens, Howie Schultz and Gene Hermanski were particularly enlightening. I also spoke with a number of other Robinson observers, writers and historians.

I was fortunate that others have previously conducted so many interviews with many of Robinson's teammates and acquaintances, including those who are no longer living. Their impressions, and those of Robinson himself, were gleaned from the above sources and books and articles about the Dodgers, Robinson, and the history of African-American baseball. A more detailed listing of sources appears in the bibliography.

Glenn Stout
September 1, 1996
Uxbridge, Massachusetts

BEGINNINGS: 1919-1941

Jackie Robinson helped change the face of twentieth century America. Yet he was born and raised in a nation still firmly entrenched in the prejudices of an earlier age. Robinson's personal journey both echoed and foreshadowed the journey of millions of other African-Americans from the margins to the mainstream of American society.

The details of Robinson's upbringing and early life are well-known, although in many accounts the basic facts have been embellished and romanticized into a form that endows the young Robinson with a wisdom well beyond his years. Such accounts are neither incorrect nor intentionally misleading. Robinson was aware of racial prejudice at a young age, and he did feel the effects of poverty. So did all African-Americans of his generation. In this, Robinson's early life was not unique.

Robinson's mother, Mallie McGriff, and his father, Jerry Robinson, were born and raised in the Deep South, near Cairo, Georgia, about twenty miles north of Tallahassee along the Georgia/Florida border. Mallie's father had been a slave, and both she and Jerry Robinson grew up in a society in which servitude was still the operative factor in their existence. Jerry Robinson was a sharecropper on the plantation of James Sasser. Although Lincoln had freed the slaves a generation before, in the rural South the institution of sharecropping had risen to replace it. African-American sharecroppers were free only in theory.

At first, Jerry Robinson was a wage worker, laboring in Sasser's fields for a salary of only ten or twelve dollars a month. It wasn't a livable wage, and like most other wage workers, Robinson was constantly in debt to his employer. He borrowed against future earnings and received much of his pay in subsistence goods like food and housing.

Jerry met Mallie in 1903, when she was fourteen years old. Her parents were strict and reli-

Mallie Robinson is shown in the living room of the family home on Pepper Street in Pasadena with sons Mack (left) and Jackie (right) in 1944. (National Baseball Library, Cooperstown, N.Y.)

gious, and not until November of 1909—after six long years of courtship—did they allow the pair to be wed.

The couple lived on Sasser's plantation. Robinson worked hard, and eventually became a "half cropper." He worked a specific plot of Sasser's land, delivered most of his crop back to Sasser, yet kept a portion to feed his family and sell for a small profit. It was still servitude, but it gave Robinson a measure of independence and the dim hope that someday he might be able to buy his own farm land and work for himself.

This was important, because his family was growing. Edgar, their first child, was born soon after Jerry and Mallie married, followed closely by Frank, Mack, and Willa Mae. Another child died in infancy.

Unfortunately for his family, while half-cropping enabled Jerry to provide for his family and even left a little extra, Robinson didn't save the money. He was tired of farming and family life, so he started spending time in Cairo, using his newfound affluence to carouse and flirt.

Jack Roosevelt Robinson was born on January 31, 1919. It was a difficult birth, Mallie's first with a doctor in attendance. She hoped the addition of another child would help keep Jerry at home, but his journeys into town only increased, and she heard rumors of his infidelity. In July, he announced that he was going to visit his brother in Texas, get established at some undefined new job, then send for the family. He left on July 28, 1919.

He never made it to Texas, traveling instead to Florida with another man's wife, never to return. Mallie Robinson was on her own, and she became the dominant figure in young Jackie Robinson's life; an ongoing example to her children of what hard work and determination could accomplish.

Her family tried to help the older children tend to the half crop, but Jim Sasser was less than understanding. Without Jerry Robinson's labor,

the family was a burden, so Sasser moved them out of their small house into a ramshackle cabin. They were worse off than ever before.

Mallie's brother Burton offered a way out. He had served as a cook for a local doctor. When the doctor joined the Army during the Great War, he brought Burton with him. The doctor was stationed in California for a time, and after the war Burton returned and settled there. On a visit back home, he regaled Mallie and other members of his clan with tales of California. There he found opportunities for work and wealth that were unthinkable for a black family in rural Georgia.

Mallie sold her family's few belongings and on May 21, 1920, she and her children boarded a train for California. In the next decade, thousands of other black families from the rural South embarked on similar journeys either west or north, marking the first full-scale black exodus from the South since the end of the Civil War.

The Robinson's experience in California was similar to that of new immigrants anywhere. And as African-Americans in Los Angeles, that's what they were, immigrants. Unlike the larger cities of the South or East, the existing African-American community in Los Angeles was small. Although the Robinsons had been born and raised in the United States, they were the ultimate outsiders in their new community. Other European immigrant groups—even the Japanese and Mexicans—were better established.

California wasn't paradise, but neither was it the South. California was segregated, but blacks were less restricted. The schools were integrated and the economy was booming. Work could be found, and opportunity created. At first, the Robinsons moved into a small apartment they shared with Burton McGriff, Mallie's sister, her family and assorted other nephews and cousins. Mallie got a job as a domestic, received some help from the local welfare office, and in 1923 purchased a small house in Pasadena on Pepper Street.

Although the Robinsons had escaped the abject poverty and institutionalized racism of the rural South, as black Americans they were still on the fringe of society and suffered the expected slights. California offered no panacea for racism.

Upon moving into their new home, Mallie quickly learned that they were the only black family in the neighborhood. Some neighbors complained to the police any time they saw the children on the street, inventing rock-throwing incidents and other acts of petty vandalism that they blamed on the Robinson boys. Others mobilized and tried to force the Robinsons out, passing around a petition that made their feelings clear. On at least one occasion, a cross was burned in front of the house.

Mallie Robinson was not swayed. She refused to move. A last ditch effort to buy the Robinsons out failed when some wealthier neighbors, whose financial support was critical to the plan, backed the Robinson's right to live there and refused to join in. Pepper Street would remain their home.

While his mother worked, Jackie tagged along to school with Willa Mae, playing outside by himself while his sister watched him from a classroom window. Although there were few other African-Americans at Grover Cleveland School, the Robinsons weren't the only minorities in town: Japanese and Mexican families were moving into the neighborhood as well.

Before entering school himself, Jackie contracted diphtheria, and nearly died. He recovered from the illness and soon followed the path of so many other children of immigrants. He fell in love with sports. Only an average student in school, in the streets and playgrounds of Pasadena young Jackie Robinson discovered that his physical talents allowed him to stand out. At an early age, he discovered the benefits of his own athletic prowess.

While still in grammar school, he sometimes came home with pocket change or an extra lunch because his more affluent, white classmates bribed Jackie to play on their side in playground games. While Robinson accepted their payoffs, he also learned that his acceptance was predicated entirely upon his athleticism. When the game ended, so too did the friendships.

Away from school, Jackie tagged along after his older brothers, playing football, basketball, baseball and running foot races along the streets. In competition with his brothers and their older, larger friends, Jackie learned that speed and quickness were his greatest allies. His physical talents developed quickly as he strove to keep up.

Family responsibilities, however, did not end at the end of the school day. All the Robinson children worked as soon as they were able. Jackie held a series of jobs, delivering newspapers, shining shoes, selling hot dogs and the like. He also indulged in some not-so-wholesome activities designed for financial gain, such as stealing errant golf balls from a nearby golf course and selling them back to club members, gambling with cards and dice and occasionally taking part in petty crimes.

He ran with an interracial group of African-American, Japanese, Mexican and Caucasian boys that called themselves the "Pepper Street Gang," united by their neighborhood ties and poverty. Many, but not all, of the group's activities involved sports. They traveled in and around Pasadena, challenging other, predominantly white groups of boys to games of football or other sports for small amounts of money. While the group shared little in common with the gangs that populate the inner city today, they occasionally broke the law and were routinely harassed by the authorities. As an adolescent and teenager, Robinson had his share of run-ins with the local police.

Yet by venturing into parts of the city that

Robinson's class at Washington Junior High Scool in 1935. He is standing in the back row on the right side. (National Baseball Library, Cooperstown, N.Y.)

were otherwise closed to him, Robinson learned valuable lessons. On the playground, playing sports, he knew he was the equal of both whites and those more affluent than he. He learned to stand up for himself and not be intimidated.

Robinson differed from his peers. The stolid example of his mother instilled him with pride. When faced with taunts or bullying because of his race, Jackie Robinson did not back down from confrontation. He reacted with confident defiance, and even earned the reputation of being arrogant. Whites thought him "uppity." In today's parlance, Robinson had attitude.

Like so many other American boys who grew up poor in urban America, ostracized by their backgrounds, sports became a way out. On the playground and in the schoolyard, in the midst of competition, the Robinson boys were momentarily able to escape the tyranny of the racial epithet. They were treated as equals, and sometimes, even the better of their peers. Edgar excelled at softball and bicycling. Frank was a talented sprinter. Mack was a fine all-around athlete, and the first of the brothers to use athletics to change the path of his life. Willa Mae was no less talented, earn-

ing letters at school in basketball, track and soccer.

The Robinsons were not unlike another family of talented athletes several hundred miles to the north in San Francisco, the DiMaggios. Oldest brothers Tom and Michael DiMaggio gave up on their dreams of athletic glory in order to help support the family, working on their father's fishing boat. Similarly, Edgar and Frank abandoned their own dreams to work and improve the lot of their family. And just as the elder DiMaggio's sacrifices enabled first Vince, then Joe and Dominic the economic freedom to pursue their game of choice, baseball, Edgar and Frank's sacrifice gave Mack and Jackie the freedom to play.

Mack Robinson, a member of the Pepper Street Gang before Jackie, was the first brother to take sports seriously. At the time, professional boxing was virtually the only sport open to African-Americans, so Mack decided to lace up the gloves. He went into training, but soon discovered that he did not enjoy being hit in the face, so he abandoned boxing for the more civilized sport of track and field.

In high school Mack was a virtual one-man

track team. He hoped to win a college scholarship, but scholarships for African-American athletes were uncommon. Despite the Depression, the combined income of Mallie Robinson and her two oldest sons enabled Mack to enroll in nearby Pasadena Junior College.

He was just as successful there as he had been in high school. Mack set a national junior college record in the long jump and won a host of sprinting titles. It wasn't easy for Mack. While African-American athletes, as a rule, were not officially banned from participating in intercollegiate or prep athletic competition in California, they weren't exactly welcomed. It wasn't enough to be good; there were plenty of good white athletes. As an African-American, Mack had to be great. Despite a heart murmur that worried doctors, Mack Robinson was a great athlete. After two years at PJC, the University of Oregon offered Mack an athletic scholarship.

Jackie followed the trail first blazed by his older brother. At Washington Junior High School, he played football, baseball, basketball and track, leading his team to championships in each sport. He even entered, and won, a city-wide ping-pong tournament. When he entered Muir Technical High School in the wake of his older brother, he quickly established himself as the better all-around athlete. For while Mack's achievements had been primarily in track and field, Jackie excelled at everything. He had speed and agility far beyond his peers; skills that served him as well in football and basketball as they did in track and baseball.

On the baseball diamond at Muir, Jackie played catcher. Although he earned a spot on a state all-star team, baseball was clearly his least favorite sport and the one which later gave him the most difficulty.

Then again, Robinson wasn't looking to make a career out of baseball or any other sport, at least not as a professional player. Apart from Negro baseball leagues, the odd barnstorming black semi-pro basketball team and the occasional black player in the professional Pacific Coast Football League, there was virtually no way for an African-American to earn a living participating in any sport except boxing. Robinson knew this. When pressed by his family to reveal his future plans, he'd say he planned to be a coach.

If Jackie was not yet fully aware of the obstacles he faced as an African-American athlete, he received an education courtesy of Mack Robinson's experience during and after the 1936 Olympic Games. For while the 1936 Games were held in racist Nazi Germany, the racism inherent in the activities of the United States Olympic Committee had a far greater impact on the team than anything the Nazis did. As fellow Olympian Louise Stokes put it before the Games, "I feel I have more to fear from my own countrymen than from Nazi Olympic officials."

Although a handful of African-Americans had competed in earlier Olympic Games, not until 1932, when six African-Americans made the U.S. team, did they make a significant impact. Sprinter Eddie Tolan won gold medals in both the 100-meter and 200-meter sprints, Ralph Metcalfe collected a silver and bronze in the same events and Edward Gordon won the long jump.

But that same year, sprinters Tidye Pickett of Chicago and Louise Stokes of Medford, Massachusetts—the first two African-American females to make the U.S. team—were not allowed to compete. They were pulled off the track because the USOC was concerned about offending stars like Babe Didrickson (whose wealthy backers heavily influenced the make-up of the squad), and also feared the fallout from Eddie Tolan's success. These backers traveled with the team and lobbied for their athletes at the expense of the unfunded Stokes and Pickett. Meanwhile, Tolan's wins made team officials wary of too much success by the team's black members, making the removal of Stokes and Pickett even more expedient.

In 1936, ten African-Americans, led by Jesse Owens, made the U.S. team. Mack Robinson qualified in the 200-meter sprint, but Owens was the star of the Games, winning the 100- and 200-meter sprints and the long jump. Mack Robinson won a silver medal, finishing second to Owens in the 200.

The final sprint event was the 400-meter relay. The U.S. team originally included Sam Stoller and Marty Glickman, both of whom were Jewish. Cowardly USOC officials feared that allowing Stoller and Glickman to compete would offend the Nazis. Besides, Owens had a chance to win a fourth medal, so they dropped Stoller and Glickman from the team in favor of Owens and Ralph Metcalfe. The U.S. team won, capturing a fourth gold for Owens.

However, the addition of the two African-Americans to the relay team threw the racial balance of the U.S. team out of kilter. To appease both the Nazis and some racist U.S. officials, Louise Stokes and Tidye Pickett were again pulled off the track and replaced by white runners. These incidents were barely acknowledged at the time and are hardly recognized today. But African-American Olympic team members, including Mack Robinson, were well aware of what went on. The lesson was clear. No matter how talented, African-American athletes were always treated first as African-Americans. No measure of achievement could overcome the color of one's skin.

That truth was reinforced by the reception Mack Robinson received when he returned home to Pasadena: there was none. Unlike today, Olympic success did not include any guarantees of financial success. Even the great Jesse Owens was soon reduced to racing against horses to earn a living. When Mack Robinson returned to Pasadena, he was all but ignored. He finally got a job as a laborer with the City of Pasadena, only to be fired along with all other blacks employed by the city in response to a judge's order to end segregation at the municipal pool.

Jackie's experience during and after his senior year at Muir reinforced those lessons. His older brother Edgar acted as something of a surrogate father to Jackie and attended all of his games. He lobbied college recruiters for Jackie's benefit. He hoped his incessant tub-thumping would help Jackie secure a college scholarship.

Although Robinson wasn't the first African-American to compete for Muir, opponents and fans from other schools weren't beyond taunting Robinson and trying to goad him into losing his cool. Indeed, when playing a team that included Robinson, the competition tried everything to get him out of the game. His final high school football game provides a clear example. Muir Tech played arch-rival Glendale in their league championship game at the Rose Bowl. During the regular season, Robinson handled the ball on nearly every possession for Muir, passing and running the ball from tailback on offense, playing safety on defense, and returning punts and kickoffs.

Robinson took the opening kickoff and was swarmed over after a short gain. Yet as he rose to his feet, a Glendale player flattened him again, hoping to get under Robinson's skin and send a message.

The message included two broken ribs and forced Robinson out of the game. Without Jackie, Muir lost, 19-0. Had Robinson committed a similar infringement, he'd have surely been disciplined. As it was, his opponent went unpunished.

Jackie was no more fortunate than Mack. While he was clearly talented, he earned the reputation of being "cocky," a euphemism meaning Robinson didn't behave with the subservient attitude coaches expected from African-Americans. Players of far lesser ability received scholarships while Robinson was ignored. Any chance Robinson had for a scholarship likely disappeared with his rib injury.

Robinson graduated from high school in 1937. At his mother's insistence, and over his own objections to adding to the family's financial burden, he enrolled in Pasadena Junior College.

Young Robinson had no illusions concerning the value of his education. While his mother wanted him to become a doctor or lawyer, Robinson majored in physical education. He was in college for one reason—to play sports.

In the fall of 1937 he went out for the football team. But in his very first practice he broke his ankle when another player rolled over it after a tackle. Jackie sat out half the season before returning for Pasadena's final six games. Without Robinson, the team struggled and lost four in a row. With him, they won five games and tied a sixth.

His ankle fully recovered, Robinson moved onto the basketball team. He was an immediate star, leading the team in scoring and finding himself the focus of the opponent's defense.

Again, Robinson's skin color made him the target of abuse. In one game against Long Beach, an opposing player named Sam Babich taunted and hacked Robinson all game long. Jackie responded in kind, and as the *Pasadena Chronicle* reported, "the two continually fouled each other all through the last half and at the conclusion of the game, had it out.

"Babich walked over to Robinson, asked him if he wanted to make something of it, and when Jackie naturally said 'Sure,' lashed out with a right hook that landed just over Robinson's eye. The next moment Babich was lying on the floor . . . and sporadic fighting had broken out all over the gym." After the fight was over, Robinson was willing to shake hands and forget the whole thing, but Babich refused.

Again, at PJC Jackie Robinson wasn't the only

Mack Robinson (left) and Jesse Owens (right) at the 1936 Berlin Olympics. Robinson would finish second behind Owens in the 200-meter dash. (National Archives)

African-American playing sports, and PJC's opponents sometimes included blacks, but no African-American had been as dominant in so many sports as Robinson. Even at this stage of his career, this made him both a target and an example, a situation that would be repeated many times over for the remainder of this life.

At the end of basketball season Robinson moved right on to baseball and track. On at least one occasion, he competed in both sports on the same day. In Pomona, site of the conference track and field championships, cooperative officials allowed Robinson to compete early in his specialty, the long jump, then he raced to the ballfield in Glendale for a baseball game.

Jackie bettered Mack's national junior college record with a leap of twenty-five feet, six and a half inches. On the baseball diamond he led PJC to the league championship while playing shortstop, hitting .417 and stealing a reported twenty-five bases in only twenty-four games. He also got his first taste of major league competition. In March of 1938, the Chicago White Sox played the PJC baseball team in an exhibition game to help raise funds for the school's athletic program. Robinson reportedly slapped out two hits and made several dazzling defensive plays at short-stop, allegedly leading White Sox Manager Jimmy Dykes to pronounce, "If that kid was white, I'd sign him now."

Jackie Robinson's collegiate career was off to a prodigious start, even if it was only junior college competition. In his sophomore year, Robinson proved he was no fluke. On the football field, he was unstoppable, leading PJC to eleven straight wins, running for more than one thousand yards—many of them on long, broken field scampers—and scoring seventeen touchdowns. In the season finale against Compton at the Rose Bowl before 30,000 fans, Robinson made the play of the game, returning a kickoff 104 yards for a touchdown.

He continued his magic on the basketball court, averaging an astounding 19 points per game in an era when teams rarely scored as many as fifty. He earned all-state honors and led the squad to the California Junior College Championship. In the spring, he again paced the baseball team to their league title and was named Southern California Junior College MVP. And he still had time to compete in the long jump and sprints in track.

Now he had the attention of the major colleges on the West Coast. Then, as now, larger schools were not averse to offering young phenoms like Robinson the moon and the stars—girls, apartments, and cars—in exchange for their athletic potential.

Jackie discussed his options with his mother and brother Frank and turned down those questionable proposals. When UCLA offered him a scholarship, Robinson took his brother's advice

and accepted. Frank reasoned that if Jackie played football in L.A., when he graduated he might be able to parlay his football fame into a job. Besides, staying close to home would allow him to perform in front of his family.

What should have been a happy time turned tragic. On May 10, 1938, just as Robinson's final year at PJC was winding down, Frank wrecked his motorcycle and was hospitalized. He died the following day.

Jackie's troubles continued in the summer of 1938. While riding in a car with some friends, another driver cut them off. Robinson's friend pursued the other car, caught up to it at a stop light, and confronted the driver. There was only one problem: the other driver was white. The sight of a young black man arguing with an older white man captured people's attention. Soon the intersection was jammed with onlookers. The police arrived, saw Robinson in the middle of the altercation, and arrested him for blocking the sidewalk, not realizing that Jackie was playing peacemaker.

Jackie's baseball coach at PJC bailed him out of jail and told him to forget the whole thing, that the authorities would surely drop the charges. Robinson took the advice.

When he entered UCLA in the fall, Jackie joined the Bruins football team. They had recruited him to pair in the Bruins backfield with star Kenny Washington. The African-American Washington starred on both sides of the line, and the team's offense depended on his running and passing ability. Because he was the Bruins main offensive threat, opponents had keyed on Washington during his first two years at UCLA. But apart from Washington and receiver Woody Strode, UCLA's offense posed few threats. The Bruins hoped Robinson would change that.

Jackie got off to a slow start in the Bruins opener, a 6-2 win over Texas Christian. A week later he made up for it against Washington, returning a punt 65 yards to set up the winning score in the 14-7 UCLA victory.

Then Robinson learned a lesson in the power of the press. His court day came up from the traffic incident, and he was again assured that the charges would be dropped. They weren't. At the hearing a judge ruled that Robinson would have to forfeit his $25 bond. It wasn't a story, except that it happened to Jackie Robinson. The local press played the story up, giving it far more attention than it deserved. Played out in the newspaper, it left the impression that Robinson was arrogant, aloof, and something of a hothead, characterizations that stayed with him throughout his career at UCLA and beyond. More than a small tinge of racism colored those reports.

The incident didn't affect him on the field, where he continued to shine. The Bruins used Robinson wisely. He was a decoy, which maximized his effectiveness. Defenses usually keyed on Washington, who handled the ball on almost every play, running inside, making a lateral, handing the ball off or passing. When they shut him down, the Bruins put the ball in Robinson's hands on the outside, forcing the defense to spread out and giving Washington room to maneuver. Robinson also returned kickoffs and teamed with Washington in the defensive backfield.

For the first time in his collegiate career, Kenny Washington had some help. He responded by running and passing for over one hundred yards nearly every game. As a result, Robinson usually touched the ball only eight or ten times a game. But when he did, he was amazing.

Against Stanford, the Bruins trailed by a touchdown with only six minutes remaining. Then Robinson intercepted a Frankie Albert pass and ran, according to the *L.A .Times*, "like his pants [were] afire." He returned the ball 49 yards before Albert chased him down, setting up the tying score. Against Oregon he scored on an 82-yard run, and caught another scoring pass from Kenny Washington, after which, the Times reported "[he] looked like a jitterbug contest. Jackie ducked, dodged, stopped short, pivoted . . . and jogged across the goal while thousands rubbed their eyes in amazement." Robinson was the difference in the win.

However, when Washington didn't need his help, Robinson was left out of the offense. In a victory over Montana, he never touched the ball. In mid-season, he sprained a knee in practice and sat out two games. Without Robinson, Washington had to do it all himself for his team to stand a chance to win. He ran for 141 yards and passed for 133 more in a 20-7 win over California, but the next week Santa Clara battled UCLA to a scoreless tie. Robinson returned to the lineup in a 13-13 tie with Oregon State, and the Bruins entered the season finale against USC with a 6-0-3 record. The Trojans, meanwhile, were also undefeated, their record marred by only two ties. To earn a trip to the Rose Bowl, UCLA had to win.

It was not to be. Before 103,000 fans at the Rose Bowl, the Trojans kept both Robinson and Washington in check and hung on for a 0-0 tie.

Statistically, Robinson had a spectacular season. He led the nation with an average of 12.24 yards per carry from the line of scrimmage, and in the Pacific Coast Conference, he finished tenth in total offense, third in rushing and second in punt returns.

Jackie Robinson was a very good football player. But many of his accomplishments that season depended upon Kenny Washington, the one great player on the Bruin squad. Washington led the entire nation in total yards, nudging out Michigan-great Tom Harmon. He ran with power and teamed with receiver Woody Strode to form one of the most dangerous pass combinations in college football. Much of Robinson's success was due to the attention the opposition was forced to pay to Washington.

Robinson became the first four letter winner in UCLA history as he achieved varsity status with the baseball, football, basketball and track teams. (National Baseball Library, Cooperstown, N.Y.)

Robinson's athletic prowess was evident in everything his did on the gridiron for UCLA.
(National Baseball Library, Cooperstown, N.Y.)

Admittedly, Robinson was a spectacular runner in the open field. Stanford Coach Tiny Thornhill called him, "the greatest backfield runner I have seen in all my connection with football." Yet Robinson lacked Washington's power, size and all-around ability. Robinson was a great player on a great team. Washington was a great player on any team.

After football season, Jackie joined the Bruins basketball team. In the highly structured, slow-paced style of play that marked the era, Robinson's athleticism made him a standout. He was nearly a one-man team, the lone star on an otherwise mediocre squad. He led the Pacific Coast Conference's Southern Division with 148 points in 12 games, including a single game high of twenty-three.

In March of 1940, Robinson had to choose between track and baseball. Because of the travel involved and increased practice time in both sports, there was virtually no way for him to compete in both at UCLA. Robinson made only a single track meet before deciding to play baseball, promising to return to the track team when baseball season ended.

As usual, he began the season in spectacular fashion. In a 6-4 Bruins loss to Los Angeles City College, he banged out four hits, stole four bases—including home—and played an errorless game in the field. He appeared as dominant on the diamond as he was on the gridiron or hardwood. Then the Bruins began to play in the California Intercollegiate Baseball Association; a league that included western powerhouses USC and St. Mary's, plus Stanford, California and Santa Clara. Now no one was calling Jackie Robinson a baseball star. He didn't hit, he didn't field, and since he wasn't getting on base, he didn't steal. The jump from junior college to major college competition was apparently too much. For the first time in his life, Jackie Robinson found a sport he couldn't play.

Plagued by poor defense and an inconsistent hitting attack, the Bruins baseball team wasn't very good. Robinson bounced all over the batting order, but he didn't produce anywhere. The only other decent game he played all year was in an exhibition against a Marine team from San Diego. In that contest, a 15-3 UCLA win, Robinson beat out three bunts, doubled, and stole three bases.

The Bruins ended the season with a 6-9 record. Robinson's final statistics were even worse. Oddly, his collegiate baseball record has rarely been scrutinized. Robinson ignores his baseball career at UCLA in his own works, and in most other presentations it is barely mentioned. One can only assume this is because his record is so contrary to Robinson's later performance on the ballfield that observers either failed to uncover it, refused to believe it, or chose to dismiss it as an anomaly. Yet it provides a valuable measuring stick against which to gauge his later achievements.

Years later, some Robinson observers said that,

If the NBA had existed at the time Robinson left UCLA it is likely he would have explored a pro basketball career. At the time this photo was taken Robinson was already a nationally recognized figure in the African-American press.

(National Baseball Library, Cooperstown, N.Y.)

Jackie finished high school as a star athlete then later distinguished himself as an athlete at UCLA. (Courtesy Boston Herald)

had Robinson been white, he'd have been signed to a professional baseball contract out of UCLA. That may have been true of his junior college career, but his performance while at UCLA states otherwise. According to documents provided by the UCLA Sports Information office and confirmed by box scores from the *L.A. Times*, in 62 at-bats during the 1940 season, Robinson collected only six hits, an average of .097, with only nine runs scored, one home run and one RBI. In the field, he made ten errors and had a fielding percentage of .907. He could hardly have played worse.

More disturbing is the fact that the level of play in college baseball on the West Coast lagged far behind that of the East and Midwest. USC and St. Mary's had sent a number of players into professional baseball, but not nearly as many as eastern powers like Notre Dame, Holy Cross, and Brown. Robinson did not just play poorly. He played poorly against sub-par competition. Even if Jackie had been white, a more unlikely candidate for the major leagues is difficult to imagine.

As soon as baseball season ended, Robinson rejoined the UCLA track team. He won the Pacific Coast League championship in the broad jump and captured the same title at the NCAA meet. But Robinson's athletic accomplishments did not stop there. Somehow, he found time to compete in other sports as well. In golf, he won the PCC championship. In tennis, he reached the semifinals of a national Negro tennis tournament. He ruled the ping pong tables on the UCLA campus. On Sundays, he even taught bible classes. No other collegiate athlete, not even Jim Thorpe, has ever competed in so many sports with such success. Baseball was the one sport that gave Robinson trouble. He lettered in football, basketball, baseball and track his first year at UCLA, the first player ever to do so. Yet the most important event of his collegiate career

Robinson (left) was a standout in basketball at UCLA. He was a two-time conference scoring champion and would have surely been a first round draft choice had the NBA been in existence in the early forties. (National Baseball Library, Cooperstown, N.Y.)

may have been the day he met nursing student Rachel Isum, his future wife.

Only a few dozen African-Americans attended UCLA, so Rachel and Jackie were not strangers to each other. Yet Robinson, despite his status as a sports' star, was still shy and aloof around women. His best friend and baseball teammate, Ray Bartlett, introduced the two and they began dating.

Their relationship reveals another, more subtle problem that faced Robinson. Even among some African-Americans, he encountered discrimination due to his dark complexion. Like her parents, Rachel was relatively light-skinned. Some African-Americans have always used depth of color to enforce their own stereotypes. In an

interview after Robinson signed with the Dodgers, Rachel related a story in which her father, who was well-educated and distinctly middle-class, initially disapproved of their relationship, asking her, "What do you see in that big, ugly ape?"

Nevertheless, the relationship flourished, although Jackie clearly lacked Rachel's sophistication. Her stoic presence was crucial to his later success. Apart from a brief breakup while Robinson was stationed in Texas in the Army, they were together for the remainder of Jackie Robinson's life.

Robinson the athlete was less successful during his final year at UCLA. He took over Kenny Washington's spot in the UCLA backfield, but without Washington's inside running ability, passing arm, and a decoy of his own to spread out the defense, Jackie found himself under unrelenting pressure. The team finished with a miserable 1-9 record.

Robinson still played well, finishing second in the PCC in total offense. He was most effective in the open field, as he averaged a stunning 21 yards per punt return. He was the entire offense in UCLA's lone win, a 34-26 spanking of Washington State, as he passed for one touchdown and ran 60 and 75 yards for two more. But for the season, his rushing average dropped from twelve to just over three yards per carry.

The Bruins suffered a similar fate in basketball. Although Robinson averaged nearly 12 points per game in league contests, the squad finished 6-20, only 2-10 in league play.

The promise of another season of baseball and track was not enough to keep Robinson in school. Although he was only a few credits shy of gradua-tion, he decided to drop out. According to his own biographies, he made his decision to leave because: "I was convinced that no amount of education would help a black man get a job . . . I could see no real future in staying at college and no real future in athletics;" a curiously bitter and narrow outlook for a young man of any color. He also worried about the financial strain that remaining in college caused his mother, and he had a job offer from the National Youth Administration.

The decision still appears curious. Leaving school increased his chance of being drafted, and he had to know that without a degree his future prospects dimmed. One has to wonder if Robinson's decision to leave UCLA may have had something to do with the approach of baseball season and the frustrations of the previous spring. For baseball, the national pastime, was not yet Jackie Robinson's game.

THE CHOSEN ONE: 1941-1945

W hen Jackie Robinson left UCLA in the spring of 1941, he was twenty-two years old. As an ex-football hero, he enjoyed a measure of fame on the west coast, but he was hardly someone expected to change the course of American life. Yet he did just that.

But he had help in this revolution. From the moment he first starred on the athletic fields of Pasadena Junior College, he had a nationwide publicity agency touting his achievements: the black press.

While African-Americans were virtually invisible in the nation's mainstream, white press, the black press worked overtime to extol their accomplishments. The black sporting press, in particular, led the way. Over the next five years they would be the critical factor in determining the course of Jackie's life.

In the early 1930s, black sportswriters around the nation decided to make a concerted, organized effort to promote the fortunes of the black athlete. Their goal was no less than the integration of American society through sports. The sports editors of most of the nation's major black newspapers—Wendell Smith of the *Pittsburgh Courier*, Sam Lacy of the *Chicago Defender*, Joe Bostic of the *New York Age*, Mabrey "Doc" Kountze of the *Boston Chronicle* and others—joined together in the National Negro Newspaper All-American Association of Sports Editors, the NNNAASE. As Kountze, the founder of the group, related a decade ago, the goal of the organization was to expose the achievements of the black athlete to a wider audience, including "feeding black sports data into the white daily press to drum up support." The group selected its own all-American teams and all-conference teams from the black colleges, which they distributed nationally via the Associated Negro Press.

They also agitated for equality in sports. Major League Baseball was their main target because other pro sports were still in their infancy. At mid-century baseball, along with radio and the movies, was America's favorite leisure-time activity. The color line in organized baseball was the most visible of barriers and offered the NNNAASE the perfect forum to push its political goals. In the early 1930s Kountze and several others arranged meetings with several baseball owners and pushed for integration. Kountze met with owners Judge Fuchs of the Braves and Bob Quinn of the Red Sox and eventually broke the color line in the press box at both Braves Field and Fenway Park. Although baseball rebuffed those efforts, Kountze and the others made sure to report on the contents of their conversations. They made it impossible for the game to plead ignorance to the plight of the black ballplayer.

From the beginning of his career, the black press recognized that Jackie Robinson was unlike any other African-American athlete in the country. He was educated, proud, a product of integration and at the same time the most accomplished athlete in the nation. Before anyone else, they sensed that Robinson had the potential to carry many of their dreams forward. They made Jackie Robinson a household name in black America well before most of white America had ever heard of him. The relationship between the black press and Robinson would prove critical to the course of his life.

Robinson neither dissuaded the writers nor sought to avoid the attention. They became his friends and companions. While others saw Robinson only as an athlete, the press saw him in full dimension—it was a mutually beneficial relationship.

After quitting UCLA in the spring of 1941,

Robinson moved to the youth camp at Atascadero, halfway between L.A. and San Francisco. He played on the camp's baseball team, entertaining campers and staff, and counseled groups of troubled youngsters. As the Depression subsided, the government started to faze out many New Deal programs. In midsummer, the camp closed, and Robinson was out of work. For African-Americans, the Depression was still in effect.

He received an invitation to play in the annual *Chicago Tribune*-sponsored College All-Star game against the NFL champion Chicago Bears. The black press had served him well, and the attention they drew to his football talents resulted in the invitation. It also meant three weeks of room and board, and free transportation to and from Chicago. Robinson couldn't afford to turn it down.

Despite not playing football for nine months, Robinson quickly got back into shape. While the All-Stars were routed by the Bears 37-13 before nearly 100,000 fans at Soldiers' Field, Robinson played well, catching a touchdown pass thrown by star Boston College quarterback Charlie O'Rourke.

While many of his teammates could look forward to continuing their football careers in the NFL, that route was closed to Robinson. In 1941, the NFL was as lily-white as Major League Baseball. Robinson, however, was still a big name in California. The semi-pro Los Angeles Bulldogs of the Pacific Coast Professional Football League made him an offer. The league was already integrated—Kenny Washington played in the Hollywood Stars backfield—and while the league wasn't quite NFL caliber, playing football beat looking for employment.

The Bulldogs offered Robinson $100 per game plus a job during the week. He needed the money and had little choice but to accept. Before he even joined the team, it moved to Hawaii,

Following his army stint, Robinson joined the Kansas City Monarchs of the Negro League. (Associated Press, Courtesy of the Boston Herald.)

becoming the Honolulu Bears. Robinson made the journey to Honolulu by boat with his old UCLA teammate Ray Bartlett.

The two men roomed together in a small apartment, worked a construction job secured by the club during the day then practiced and played at night. Robinson performed well, but grew tired of the long hours and the distance between him and Rachel.

He left Hawaii on December 5, and was at sea when Pearl Harbor was bombed. Now the war hung over everything. Robinson had a draft deferment as sole supporter of his mother, but it was impossible for him to know how long that would last.

Jackie made it through the winter playing semi-pro basketball for the Los Angeles Red Devils, but his earnings amounted to little more than pocket change. He still wanted to coach, but

civilian jobs of any kind were hard to come by for a black man in America. Besides, with the war going on, it was just a matter of time before he would be called into military service. Robinson decided not to use his support of his mother to extend his deferment and was drafted soon after. The induction orders came on March 23, 1942. One day earlier, Robinson took part in one of the most important yet least known incidents of his career.

Robinson had always been a familiar figure at Pasadena's Brookfield Park, and the spring of 1942 was no different. He was at the park nearly every day, playing softball and an occasional baseball game—even appearing with a touring black team against major league pitcher Red Ruffing's all stars—impressing everyone with his athletic skill.

Brookfield Park was also the wartime spring

Robinson was one of thousands of African-Americans to serve in the military during the second World War. When Baseball Commissioner Albert "Happy" Chandler decided that Robinson would be allowed to play organized baseball he reasoned, as did most Americans, that if blacks could die for their country they could also play the National Pastime. (Courtest Boston Herald)

training site of the Chicago White Sox. On March 22, Robinson and Nate Moreland, an African-American pitcher who had pitched for Tampico in the Mexican League the year before, were invited to a tryout.

Precisely how the two men received the invitation is not clear. But the *Daily Worker*, the official newspaper of the Communist Party of the United States, was the only paper to report on the tryout and the only paper outside the black community to make the integration of baseball a cause. In all likelihood, the *Worker* arranged for the tryout, which also explains why Robinson never mentioned it again.

According to the *Worker*, which headlined the story on the back page, the White Sox were impressed with both players. Chicago Manager Jimmy Dykes was quoted as telling the players that, "Personally, I would welcome Negro players on the Sox, and I believe that every one of the other fifteen big league managers would do likewise." He added that he believed Robinson was worth $50,000 to any big league club. Later in the same article, Cincinnati Reds Manager Bill McKechnie and Dodgers Manager Leo Durocher were quoted supporting the efforts to integrate baseball.

While it is unlikely the tryout was serious, at the same time it was not insignificant. For the first time, black players had been invited to perform before a big league manager at a big league camp. The choice of Jackie Robinson as one of those two players was not accidental. The *Worker* enjoyed a good relationship with the black press, and it is likely that Robinson was chosen for the tryout due to his high profile. Already the black press had pegged him as a possible choice to bring down the color bar.

A draft notice the next day made the question moot. Robinson was inducted into the Army on April 3, 1942.

He went through basic training at Fort Riley,

Robinson achieved the rank of second lieutenant in the United States Army. (National Baseball Library, Cooperstown, N.Y.)

Kansas. There he received a fast lesson in racism in the American military. If Robinson was not politicized before he entered the Army, he was by the time he left. Like other African-American soldiers, he was assigned to a segregated unit, the Cavalry, and spent his time caring for horses and mucking stalls. He applied to Officer Candidate School, but was turned down.

Robinson wasn't just some faceless soldier. Heavyweight champ Joe Louis was assigned to Riley, and he knew who Robinson was. When Jackie told the boxer of his inability to gain admittance into officer's school, Louis, perhaps the only black soldier in America with anything resembling "pull," interceded. Robinson was soon accepted to OCS and became a morale officer for a unit of black soldiers. He soon learned just exactly how difficult it was to be a black soldier in the American Army and have any morale whatsoever.

In the spring of 1943, he naively tried to join the base baseball team, a crack squad whose members included Pete Reiser and Dixie Walker, both of whom would later be teammates with Robinson on the Dodgers. An officer approached him and told him he would have to play for the colored team.

But there was no colored team. A demeaned Robinson walked off the field alone.

Jackie took his revenge the following fall. Robinson's football skills were well known, and now the Army brass wanted him to play football on the camp team. But they made the mistake of telling Robinson he wouldn't be allowed to play when the team faced squads from the South.

That was all Robinson needed to hear: he quit the team.

Meanwhile, he was developing a reputation. Increasingly, Robinson stood up to the racism of the Army. He backed his men to the hilt, which rankled white officers. They responded by sending him farther south, to Fort Hood, Texas.

From Fort Hood, most soldiers went directly overseas. Robinson was transferred into an all-black tank battalion and became a platoon leader.

Two significant events marked his experience at Fort Hood, both of which were key to his later experiences. In the first, Robinson started playing ball again. He organized a battalion baseball team, and pitched on the officer's fast-pitch softball team.

After being away from the game for more than two years, the opportunity to play ball again allowed Robinson to keep his skills sharp. Had he not created his own opportunity to play, one wonders if he ever would have considered resuming his baseball career after leaving the Army. Unlike football, which is more dependent on speed and instinct, baseball is a game of timing. Robinson was able to work off some of the rust that had built up since he last played that day at Brookfield Park.

The second event is better known, and has even been the subject of a feature film. On the evening of July 6, 1944 Robinson boarded a bus at Camp Hood. When he stepped off a few moments later, his military career was all but over.

Buses were segregated on base. Not only did black soldiers have to sit in the back, but they were routinely removed in favor of whites if the buses became overcrowded. When Robinson boarded the bus, he took a seat in the middle next to a light-skinned black woman, a fellow officer's wife. The bus driver, believing the woman was white, stopped the bus and asked Robinson to move to the back. Robinson refused. The driver then demanded that Robinson leave the bus altogether. He refused again. The two men argued, and the bus driver returned the bus back to the depot, where Robinson was taken into custody by MPs.

Robinson was charged with insubordination and faced three separate charges for a general court-martial. But the army soon learned that Jackie Robinson was not a run-of-the-mill soldier.

The black press got involved. Within a few weeks the Robinson case made him a cause celebre. Robinson's white battalion commander backed him and refused to sign the papers needed for the court martial. The Army responded by transferring Robinson to another unit whose commanding officer would sign.

Robinson's notoriety eventually helped him earn an acquittal, but his military career was ruined. He was transferred several times and the Army suddenly took a great interest in the ankle he had broken nearly a decade before, finally deciding, with no discouragement from Robinson, that it might interfere with his responsibilities.

On November 28 in Camp Breckinridge, Kentucky, Robinson was "honorably relieved from active duty . . . by reason of physical disqualification." The result was that Jackie Robinson needed to find a job.

He was not entirely without prospects. He had made ends meet in the past by playing football and basketball. But with the onset of winter, football season was over and basketball wasn't very lucrative. Jackie Robinson was already thinking about baseball.

Precisely how Robinson came to play for the Kansas City Monarchs is unclear. Robinson claimed he met Monarchs pitcher Ted Alexander at Camp Breckinridge, and that Alexander suggested he write to the Monarchs for a tryout. But Monarchs pitcher Hilton Smith later claimed it was he, and not Alexander, who arranged for Robinson to be invited for a tryout.

No matter. Whatever the surrounding circumstances, Robinson was attractive to Negro League baseball. He was already one of the best known African-American athletes in the country. His experience in the military made him even more famous and a hero to many. If he could still play, he would immediately become one of the most visible players in Negro League baseball.

Spring was still several months away, so with the help of Karl Downs, an old minister friend from Pasadena, Robinson became basketball coach at tiny all-black Sam Houston College in Huntsville, Texas. Drawing on a student body of fewer than fifty young men, Robinson nonetheless put together a competitive team. Yet the coaching stint was just a stopgap measure designed to carry him until the spring. At some point that winter, Robinson wrote the Monarchs and requested a tryout. He was told to report to camp in Houston, Texas in March of 1945.

The Kansas City Monarchs were the most storied franchise in Negro League baseball. Paced by pitcher Satchel Paige, by far the most famous black player in America, the Monarchs enjoyed a nationwide reputation. No other Negro League team, not even the Homestead Grays of Josh Gibson and Buck Leonard, was as popular as the Monarchs. Because of Paige, the Monarchs were the most sought after Negro League team on the barnstorming circuit. As such, the Monarchs performance in "official" Negro American League games sometimes didn't matter as much as exhibitions against white teams. Paige rarely performed during the regular season, saving his arm for the more lucrative exhibitions.

The 1945 Monarchs weren't quite the powerhouse of years past. After winning pennants in the Negro American League from 1939 thru 1942, the Monarchs fell on hard times. Like Major League Baseball, the Negro Leagues were decimated by the war. Hundreds of talented players were in military service, and rosters were filled with either aging veterans or untried youngsters. In 1944 the Monarchs sometimes fielded as few as nine players, and finished last in NAL.

Jackie Robinson was the right man at the right time. He joined the Monarchs at a time when they were desperate for talent and the Negro Leagues were at their weakest.

Spring training for Negro League teams hardly resembled that of organized baseball. They didn't practice much, instead playing exhibition games against local teams. Monarchs Co-Owner J.L. Wilkinson assigned Robinson to an exhibition squad led by veteran infielder Newt Allen. Allen played Robinson at shortstop in a few exhibitions, then gave Wilkinson his blunt appraisal. Robinson was fast, heady, could hit a little, was a fine bunter and showed a good glove. But his arm was suspect. From shortstop, he couldn't make a strong throw from the hole. Nonetheless, Allen recommended that Robinson be placed on the team as a utility infielder.

Written contracts were almost nonexistent in Negro League baseball. Robinson verbally agreed to a salary of $400 per month, quite a bit by Negro League standards, but one that demonstrates that the Monarchs interest in Robinson probably had as much to do with his notoriety as with his ability. Despite the war, the Monarchs were well fixed in the infield. Shortstop Jesse Williams was one of the best fielding shortstops in Negro League baseball, and the other positions were covered by veterans. Robinson got lucky. Williams came down with a sore arm, and was moved to second base. None of the other infielders had enough range to play short. Robinson, by default, became the Monarchs shortstop.

The black press took immediate note of Robinson's presence on the Monarchs roster, as the *Chicago Defender* commented that the Monarchs had "put one over" on other Negro League teams by adding him to their roster. Although he had yet to play an official game, Robinson was already gathering press attention beyond what he yet deserved.

As Jackie was making his first foray into professional baseball, there was increasing dissatisfaction with organized baseball's color line, an unwritten but intransigent barrier that had kept baseball white for more than fifty years. No African-American had played in organized baseball in the twentieth century.

But fair employment legislation was pending in Congress and there was increasing pressure from a variety of groups to end Jim Crow practices in the workplace. Even some white sports writers, like Dave Egan of the *Boston Record* and Jimmy Cannon of the *New York Mirror*, were beginning to call on baseball to drop the color bar. The logic was both simple and irrefutable: If an African-American could fight and die for his country overseas, then he deserved equal treatment in the United States.

The integration of baseball began to seem inevitable. In 1944, owner Bill Veeck of the St. Louis Browns was prepared to buy the Philadelphia Phillies and stock the team with Negro League players, but Baseball Commissioner Kenesaw Mountain Landis was staunchly opposed to integration. Veeck erred by informing the commissioner of his plans in advance, and overnight Landis arranged for another man to purchase the Phillies, for much less than what Veeck was willing to pay.

Landis died shortly thereafter. Where as before there had been silence on the integration issue from the game's highest office, new Commissioner Happy Chandler, a former United States Senator from Kentucky, was intimating that perhaps it was time to drop the color bar. Some owners were saying much the same thing. No one wanted problems with Congress, which could revoke baseball's treasured antitrust exemption.

In Boston, Jewish city councilman Isadore Muchnick took up the battle. He threatened to block the annual license issued to the Braves and Red Sox to play baseball on Sunday unless they allowed blacks to play. In a letter to owners Tom Yawkey of the Red Sox and Bob Quinn of the

Robinson is shown at a tryout on March 22, 1942 with the White Sox at Brookfield Park in San Diego. This tryout was arranged after much lobbying by both the African-American press and the communist newspaper, The Daily Worker. *(National Baseball Library, Cooperstown, N.Y.)*

*Robinson impressed
scouts with his blinding
speed and was said by
Jimmy Dykes to be
worth the then-phenom-
enal sum of fifty thou-
sand dollars to the major
league club willing to
sign him.*
(National Baseball Library,
Cooperstown, N.Y.)

Braves, Muchnick summed up his argument suc-
cinctly. "I cannot understand how baseball," he
wrote, "which claims to be the national sport and
which in my opinion receives special favors and
dispensations from the Federal Government
because of alleged morale value, can continue a
pre-Civil War attitude toward American citizens
because of the color of their skin."

Muchnick's charges received wide play in the
black press. He heard back from Red Sox General
Manager Eddie Collins, who wrote that the Red
Sox would be happy to have black players but that
"none had ever asked to try out," and that Collins
believed "none wanted to play in the major
leagues" because they were better off financially
in the Negro Leagues.

At the same time, sports writer Joe Bostic of
the *New York Age* decided it was time to take
more direct action. On April 6, he arrived unan-
nounced at the Brooklyn Dodgers training camp
in Bear Mountain New York with pitcher Terris

McDuffie and first baseman Dave "Showboat"
Thomas—two Negro League veterans well past
their prime—and demanded a tryout.

Bostic had reason to think he might find a welcome reception from Dodgers President Branch
Rickey, who in the past had made several cautious
statements supporting the integration of baseball.
Recently, Rickey even announced his intention to
create a black league and field his own team, the
Brooklyn Brown Dodgers, in a move which many
interpreted as a precursor to the integration of
the Dodgers themselves.

But Bostic miscalculated. To avoid a scene,
and the accompanying bad publicity, Rickey
agreed to a cursory workout and then sent the
players on their way. Next he cornered Bostic
and berated him for putting him on the spot.
Despite later events, Rickey would never speak to
Bostic again.

Meanwhile, Robinson made his first appearance with the Monarchs on Sunday, April 1, in

Houston against a team of minor league stars. In a 14-inning, 4-4 tie, Robinson sparkled in the field, but failed to impress at the plate. A week later, he hit fifth, collected two hits and stole a base in the first game of a double-header against the Birmingham Black Barons.

Interestingly enough, the game was reported in the *Pittsburgh Courier*, which published a national edition and was read by African-Americans across the country. Robinson's performance was featured, as the anonymous author wrote, "Jackie Robinson had a big day afield and at bat . . . He drove in the first pair of Monarchs runs with a drive to left center." It was odd for a player with only a few weeks experience to get that much attention, but it demonstrates the importance the black press already attached to Jackie.

Another reason why the *Courier* wrote about Robinson became clear a week later. In consort with Muchnick, *Courier* Sports Editor Wendell Smith collected Robinson, Sam Jethroe of the Cleveland Buckeyes and Marvin Williams of the Philadelphia Stars, and traveled to Boston to confront the Red Sox. Here, Smith and Muchnick planned to announce, are three men who want to play Major League Baseball.

Jethroe and Williams were already stars. Jethroe, an outfielder, had led the Negro American League with a .353 average in 1944 and would go on to win a second title with a .393 average in 1945. Williams, a second baseman, had hit .338 in the Negro National League in 1944 and .362 for Mexico City in the winter Mexican League.

How did Robinson fit in? Smith later wrote that he had selected the three because of their performance in 1944 and because of their age, yet Robinson hadn't played anywhere in 1944 and at age twenty-six was three years older than Jethroe and four years older than Williams. Clearly, Robinson was chosen for other reasons.

While Jethroe and Williams may have possessed the requisite baseball skills, Robinson posed the requisite social skills. He was college educated and a veteran, and because of his football career he was already better known to whites than almost any Negro Leaguer other than Satchel Paige. Moreover, he had grown up and gone to school in an integrated society, was accus-

Many of Robinson's future teammates got their first glimpse of the 27-year-old rookie at the Dodgers-Royals spring training games in 1946. (National Baseball Library, Cooperstown, N.Y.)

Outfielder Sam Jethroe (left) and pitcher Dan Bankhead (right) are shown as members of the Montreal Royals. Jethroe would join Robinson in a legendary 1945 tryout at Fenway Park while Bankhead would join Robinson as a member of the Dodgers in 1947.
(Courtesy of The Boston Herald)

tomed to whites and was well spoken. One cannot help but believe that by bringing Robinson to Boston, Smith was doing his utmost to hold Robinson before the doors of baseball and make sure he was seen.

The four men spent days waiting in a Boston hotel while Muchnick petitioned both the Red Sox and Braves for a tryout. Finally, the Red Sox grudgingly acquiesced. What happened that day has since become legend.

Smith, Muchnick, and the three players arrived at Fenway Park at 10:30 on the morning of April 16, one day before the Sox were scheduled to open their season in New York. The three players changed into their Negro League uniforms and were ushered out onto the field where Coach Hugh Duffy was holding a tryout for several dozen white players. Manager Joe Cronin sat in the stands while Duffy put the players through their paces. Robinson later recalled that he hit the ball

that day "good to all fields." So did Muchnick, who remembered that "you never saw anyone hit the wall the way Robinson did that day."

The three also worked out in the field. At some point during the tryout, a voice allegedly boomed from the stands "get those niggers off the field!" The tryout was soon over.

None of the three players involved ever mentioned the outburst, and it may be apocryphal, but around Boston it has long been whispered that a member of the Boston front office was the speaker. Years later, this author conducted an interview with a gentleman named Bill Gavin, who once served as the visitor's batboy at Fenway Park. On a visit to spring training one year, he had the opportunity to ask Robinson about the tryout. When he inquired as to whether anything was yelled from the stands, a visibly upset Robinson hissed, "I played in the National League," got up and left.

The tryout went well, but although Hugh Duffy supposedly asked that the Red Sox sign Robinson, the team did nothing. Collins later told reporters that when Cronin broke his leg a few days later, any plans to sign the players went to the back burner. Cronin himself later told reporters that "They weren't ready for the majors," and that the Red Sox knew they couldn't send them to play ball in segregated Louisville, Kentucky, the Red Sox Triple-A franchise.

Still, the tryout did serve a purpose. Robinson was the one. Throughout the remainder of the season Smith took every opportunity to tout Robinson's play. Monarchs games received more play in the *Courier* than even those of the Pittsburgh-based Homestead Grays.

Wendell Smith later claimed to have contacted Rickey shortly after the Boston tryout. Smith told Rickey about Robinson, and Rickey told Smith then that he was looking for African-American talent. Rickey was unfamiliar with Robinson, but at Smith's urging he had Dodgers scouts check him out. If so, it gives credence to the huge role the black press played in the selection of Robinson. As such, it may have been just the first of many instances where Rickey leaked word of his plans to Smith in advance of any word to the mainstream press.

The relationship between Rickey and Smith is almost as fascinating as that which developed later between Rickey and Robinson. They formed a secret alliance that lasted several critical seasons early in Robinson's career. Smith served as Rickey's sounding board in the black community, his confidant concerning his plans to integrate baseball, and according to some, was later even put on the Dodgers payroll to help look after Robinson.

There are even reports that suggest Rickey met secretly with Robinson following a Monarchs game in Newark in June. If he did, such a meeting may have been premature, for Robinson was still feeling his way around the league.

While Robinson was one of the leading hitters in the Negro American League and was named to the Western team in the Negro League all-star game—where he went hitless in five at bats—not everyone was impressed. At the time, most Negro Leaguers agreed with the sentiments of Buck Leonard, who later told a reporter bluntly that, "We had a whole lot of ballplayers better than Jackie."

Despite his success, Robinson was not enamored of life in the Negro Leagues. While the money was good, the road took most of it. He was appalled at the living conditions, detested the constant travel, found fault with the fields and the umpiring, and was aloof from his own teammates. Robinson, whose West Coast upbringing and college background were unique in the Negro Leagues, had little in common with the other Monarchs players. He neither smoked nor drank, as did most of his teammates, and he frowned

Sportswriter Wendell Smith of The Pittsburgh Courier *was not only Robinson's main champion in the African-American press but also would later ghost write a column under Robinson's byline.* (National Baseball Hall of Fame)

upon many of their post-game activities. In turn, his teammates found Robinson standoffish and easily angered. They appreciated his skill and willingness to learn, but were a bit mystified by all the attention paid to him in the press and couldn't understand why Robinson had been selected for the earlier tryout. After all, he wasn't even the best player on the team, much less the best player in the Negro Leagues.

There is no doubt that Robinson benefitted from the relative weakness of the NAL that year. Beyond stating that some players were undoubtedly of major league, even Hall of Fame caliber, it is almost impossible to gauge the overall level of play in Negro League baseball. Rosters were fluid, organization almost nonexistent, scheduling inconsistent. Good players were often withheld from league games in favor of exhibitions.

Still, the weakness of the league in the war years allowed Robinson the time to regain his timing, put his game back together, and even improve upon it. The long bus rides served as a virtual school of baseball strategy, while the style of play favored in the Negro Leagues with its focus on speed played to Robinson's own strengths. He didn't just learn to play again, he learned to play better than he ever had before. Howerver, he was still erratic. In a double-header against the Grays in Washington, Robinson tied a Negro League record by bashing out seven consecutive hits, yet his poor defense led to big rallies that cost the Monarchs both games.

Yet at other times, Jackie was one of the most exciting players in Negro League baseball. In an exhibition in Boston at Braves Field against a Navy all-star team in mid-August, Robinson was the whole show. Although Satchel Paige missed the game after being beaten by a Washington D.C. traffic cop following a minor transgression, Robinson nonetheless paced the Monarchs to an 11-1 win. He cracked out two hits, stole second twice, third once, and climaxed his performance with a daring steal of home, leaving Boston fans wondering what might have been.

Branch Rickey and Leo Durocher, representing the Dodgers, were in Chicago in November of 1943 to select and trade players.
(International News Photo)

Two weeks later, Robinson received an invitation. Branch Rickey of the Brooklyn Dodgers wanted to meet with him.

Much has been written about Rickey's role in breaking baseball's color line. In most accounts of Robinson's story, it is Branch Rickey, not Jackie Robinson, who dominates. But it is important to remember that the bulk of this history has been written by those who find they have more in common with Rickey's own sense of morality than with Robinson's demonstrative courage.

Before taking over the Dodgers as president and owner of one-third of the club in 1942, Rickey had served baseball for more than forty years. He parlayed his mediocre career as a back-up catcher for the St. Louis Browns and Yankees into an undistinguished stint as manager of the Browns. He then took over the administrative reigns of the St. Louis Cardinals, where he found his true calling: developing the farm system and pioneering the nationwide use of scouts.

Rickey was many things to many people, at once complicated and flamboyant, spiritual and materialistic to a fault, vain and pious. His administrative genius earned him the nickname "the Mahatma," while his penurious nature also led some New York writers to refer to him as "El Cheapo." Rickey was equal parts innovator and despot, a pious showman who refused to attend games on Sunday and a notorious skinflint who cloaked his sometimes ruthless financial manipulations in biblical hyperbole. For every player he sold, twenty percent of the price went into his own pocket. His desire to break baseball's color line served both parts of his nature, appealing to both his egotistical sense of morality and his overwhelming concern with the bottom line. He did what he did to secure his place in history and to make money. The two cannot be separated.

According to legend, Rickey's racial awareness was first raised when he served as baseball coach at Ohio Wesleyan University. One of his players,

Pitcher John Wright and Robinson make baseball history as they enter Brooklyn spring training camp in February 1946. By the end of camp both would be assigned to Montreal of the International League. (National Baseball Library, Cooperstown, N.Y.)

first baseman Charlie Thomas, was black. The team traveled to South Bend, Indiana to play Notre Dame, and Thomas was refused admittance at the teams' hotel. Rickey eventually convinced the management to allow Thomas to stay on a cot in his room as if he were a servant. Later that night, Rickey allegedly witnessed a distraught Thomas trying to wash the blackness off his skin.

"That scene haunted me for many years," Rickey said later, "and I vowed that I would always do whatever I could to see that other Americans did not have to face the bitter humiliation that was heaped upon Charles Thomas."

Years later Thomas could recall the snub at the hotel, but had no recollection of ever trying to wash the color off his hands. And Rickey, despite the effect he later claimed the incident had upon him, took no action to rectify that inequality for

With Montreal Royals Owner Hector Racine (left) and other club officials looking on, Robinson signs his Royals contract on October 23, 1945. (Associated Press)

nearly forty years, and then only when the financial and historic benefits of doing so became pronounced.

Though Rickey may well have been bothered by prejudice, the motivating factor that finally spurred him to action was money. During the war, the Negro Leagues were highly profitable. When he took over the Dodgers, they were successful neither in the standings nor on paper. They were the only one of three New York teams that failed to reap a windfall through renting their parks to Negro League teams.

A generation before, he had started a dynasty and created a small fortune as general manager of the St. Louis Cardinals when he invented baseball's farm system. Now, in Brooklyn, Rickey sensed a similar opportunity. He sought to gain a similar advantage by making the Dodgers the first major league team to make use of black talent.

This is not to say that the morality of the situation was unimportant, but it was not until the financial benefits became apparent that Rickey took action. Quite frankly, Rickey likely made his move when he did because he was afraid he might be beaten to the punch.

Rickey wasn't naive. He knew the issue was volatile and that he had to move carefully. He neither wanted to alienate the other owners, anger the Commissioner, nor tip his hand. Initially, he may not even have been sure himself precisely what his final goal was. So in 1943 he first sent scouts into the Negro Leagues under the cover of scouting for his own black team, for the possible creation of another Negro League, or maybe, just maybe, for the Dodgers themselves. The end result was driven by the changing political climate that rapidly enveloped the racial issue in baseball as soon as the war ended.

If Rickey did not break the color line soon, that change would either be legislated or someone else would profit from the opportunity. His advantage would be lost.

According to the Rickey legend, his final selection of Robinson was the end result of a laborious process. His scouts looked at hundreds of players, directed by Rickey to look for for talent first—primarily speed, batting power, and a strong arm—and character second. Of that, Rickey would be the ultimate scout, because he was seeking not just a great player—one whose on-field success was virtually guaranteed—but a great man, one who could survive the accompanying hostilities.

How odd it is then, that this multi-year effort resulted in the selection of the very same player the black sporting press had been touting for years, the one man who had participated in two of the three tryouts that major league teams had ever held for black players. The evidence reveals that while Rickey certainly scoured the Negro Leagues for talent, once he became aware of Jackie Robinson he looked no further in regard to whom he would sign first. This suggests that to some degree Rickey's laborious search for the "right" player is revisionist hyperbole. For while, in retrospect, Robinson was undoubtedly the correct choice, he fulfilled few of Rickey's preexisting conditions. He had speed, but his arm was suspect and as yet he had demonstrated little power. He was also twenty-six, a little old to be considered a prospect, and lacked experience. Of Robinson's character, even a cursory investigation would not suggest that this was a man made to turn the other cheek: Robinson had been standing up for his rights since he could walk.

In late August, Rickey sent Clyde Sukeforth to scout Robinson in Chicago and check out his arm from shortstop. But when Sukeforth arrived in Chicago he discovered that Robinson had a sore shoulder and was temporarily out of the lineup.

He had an usher bring Robinson up into the stands to introduce himself and arranged a meeting later that day at his hotel. He told Robinson that Rickey was starting his own black league and wanted to speak with him. Sukeforth also quizzed Robinson about his background, asking why he had been discharged from the Army. Robinson answered that it was because of his old football ankle injury, a technically correct response that conveniently failed to mention the court martial. So much for Rickey's vaunted intelligence system.

Robinson and Sukeforth met a few days later in Toledo and traveled together to Brooklyn. On the morning of August 28, 1945, Jackie Robinson walked into the Dodgers offices at 215 Montague Street in Brooklyn for a gathering that changed baseball forever.

The meeting between Rickey and Robinson has since become the stuff of legend, immortalized on the screen and through repeated retelling, each of which has added to its dramatic luster.

When Dodgers scout Clyde Sukeforth first interviewed Robinson he did so under the guise that Rickey was interested in starting his own Negro League. Sukeforth later would bring Robinson to Brooklyn where he signed his historic contract on August 28, 1945.
(National Baseball Library, Cooperstown, N.Y.)

While the meeting was no doubt charged with electricity, it also may not have been quite as pivotal as it has since been described. A close examination of the published accounts of their conversation is revealing. For while the details of the meeting vary in small ways, the order of the conversation does not. Rickey clearly had already decided to sign Robinson. In many ways the conversation was a formality, not quite as significant then as it appears in retrospect.

With Clyde Sukeforth looking on, Rickey and Robinson exchanged pleasantries. Then Rickey asked Robinson if he had a girl.

A puzzled Robinson responded that he did.

Rickey then peppered Robinson with a series of questions about Rachel's background, then admonished Jackie to marry her.

The exchange is telling. For while Rickey later claimed to have thoroughly investigated Robinson, he apparently failed to uncover this most basic piece of information. The depth of his "investigation" appears overstated.

Then, significantly, Rickey asked Robinson if he were under written contract to the Monarchs, another bit of information any investigation should have uncovered. Robinson said he wasn't and Rickey then asked him if he knew why he was there. Jackie responded that Sukeforth had told him Rickey was scouting for players for his new league.

Then Rickey spilled the beans, admitting that Sukeforth had been directed to say that. The real reason Robinson was there was that Rickey wanted him to play in the Brooklyn organization.

There was no turning back now, which makes the remainder of their exchange a little less consequential than has previously been admitted. Rickey interrogated Robinson about his background, quizzing him about his past, his relationships with women, and his reputation as a troublemaker at UCLA. Then Branch began role playing, gauging Robinson's reaction as he animatedly peppered him with racial insults and acted out various racial slights.

In the most famous moment of the meeting, Robinson responded to one such insult with the words. "Mr. Rickey, what do you want? Do you want a ballplayer who is afraid to fight back?"

"I want a ballplayer with guts enough not to fight back," Rickey said.

A later exchange delivered a similar resonance. Rickey baited Robinson with a characterization of a ballplayer sliding into Robinson with spikes high, hurling racial epithets, then punching Robinson in the face. His voice booming, Rickey then asked, "What do you do now, Jackie."

Robinson understood. "I get it Mr. Rickey," he answered. "I've got another cheek."

Satisfied, Rickey made his offer formal. He pushed a contract across his desk that gave Robinson a $3,500 bonus and promised him $600 a month during the 1946 season, and included a clause in which Rickey was not liable if Robinson were under contract to any other baseball organization. Branch added that he expected Robinson to keep their pact a secret, for he didn't plan to announce the signing for several months. Robinson agreed.

When Jackie Robinson walked back out onto Montague Street, everything had changed.

A ROYAL START:
1945-1946

Branch Rickey kept the meeting a secret for less than a week. Wendell Smith broke the story in the *Courier* on September 8.

The story was a set up from the beginning, likely leaked by Rickey and written by Smith the exact way Rickey wanted it written. Smith quoted Rickey as saying he met with Robinson "to get some ideas from him" concerning Negro baseball and that "we did not discuss the possibility of Robinson becoming a member of the Brooklyn Dodgers organization." Smith left little doubt that Rickey's declaration was nothing more than a smoke screen. "It appears," he wrote, "the Brooklyn boss has a plan in his mind that extends farther than just the future of Negro baseball as an organization. Only time, it seems, will reveal what he has in mind."

That timetable is precisely what worried Rickey. The story, which acknowledged the meet-

ing and hinted at its significance, gave Rickey an opportunity to gauge reaction and do some planning, but Rickey couldn't control everything. He planned to have Arthur Mann break the story in *Look* magazine, and even had Robinson pose for some accompanying photographs, but political pressure forced his hand.

In New York, Mayor Fiorello LaGuardia's sub-committee on the integration of baseball was preparing to issue a call for New York's teams to begin signing players, and a communist candidate for New York city council was making hay with the issue.

Rickey didn't want anyone to think he was acting in response to political pressure; his ego wouldn't allow it. In late October he made hurried plans to break the news.

Meanwhile, Jackie Robinson had to act as if nothing was happening. He told Rachel and his mother of the meeting with Rickey, and while

Robinson's dynamic performance in Montreal insured that he would compete for a place in the starting lineup of the 1947 Brooklyn Dodgers. (National Baseball Library, Cooperstown, N.Y.)

many in the black press and Negro baseball were suspicious, no one wanted to risk ruining Robinson's chance.

Jackie was left to resume his life. He briefly rejoined the Monarchs, but left the team before the season ended to join the barnstorming Kansas City Royals on the West Coast. Robinson finished his single season of Negro League play with a .387 batting average, 36 runs scored, 23 RBIs and 13 stolen bases in 47 games. The Monarchs finished third in each half of the Negro American League's season, with a combined record of 32-30.

Robinson returned east in mid-October. He had signed on to barnstorm in Venezuela later that winter, and was working out at the Harlem YMCA with several other players in preparation for the trip, when he received word from Rickey to fly to Montreal.

On the morning of October 23, 1945, the Triple-A Montreal Royals of the International League announced that they would hold a press conference later that day that would affect baseball "coast to coast."

Flanked by President Hector Racine of the Royals, Vice President Romeo Gavreau, and Branch Rickey Jr., who ran his father's farm system, Robinson inked the same contract he had been offered two months before. Now it was official.

Significantly, Robinson was signed to a Montreal contract, and everything still depended upon him making the team the following spring. Speculation over bringing him up to the majors with the Dodgers was downplayed as premature. While nearly everyone saw through it, Rickey wanted Robinson's signing to appear, as much as possible, as something done by the Montreal Royals. Rickey didn't want Robinson to face any unrealistic expectations. If he were to be promoted, he needed time to prepare. Besides, as yet there was no assurance that Robinson would make the grade.

The signing sent reporters scrambling to phones and shock waves throughout baseball. Yet in their public statements most baseball men and sports writers were surprisingly diplomatic. Their real feelings were kept private. In fact, those who expressed the greatest public outrage at Robinson's signing were the men who owned teams in the Negro Leagues. Kansas City Monarchs Co-Owner Tom Baird was livid, and wanted compensation for Robinson, but the Monarchs had no written contract with Robinson, and Rickey was showing no inclination to admit the existence of either written or oral contracts in regard to Negro League players. If he did, he knew that it would hamper his ability to sign other black players in the future. Baird and the other, mostly white owners of Negro League teams, had no pull in the matter. Baird realized if he tried to block Robinson's signing in court, he'd lose out at the box office and in the black press. He let Robinson go.

Branch Rickey had surprisingly little contact with Robinson in the off-season. In November, Jackie departed for Venezuela with his barnstorming teammates, including such Negro League stars as Buck Leonard, Sam Jethroe and Roy Campanella. The trip was important. Robinson still had a lot to learn about baseball. He had probably played less than one hundred games since leaving UCLA five years before. Some of Robinson's teammates tried to take him under their wing and give him tips on how to improve

Montreal Manager Clay Hopper considered blacks to be sub-human before Robinson changed his life and the lives of many in baseball who shared his views.
(National Baseball Hall of Fame, Cooperstown, N.Y.)

Pitcher John R. Wright would join Robinson as a member of the 1945 Montreal Royals. (Photograph Courtesy of The Boston Herald)

his play, but Robinson, oddly, rebuffed their efforts. Others remained aloof, unable to understand why Robinson, of all players, had been selected to play organized baseball, a question even Robinson couldn't answer.

Even then, the announcement made Robinson the big draw on the tour. But he struggled. While the team won eighteen of twenty games and a number of players hit over .400, Robinson pressed and hit under .300.

While Jackie was in South America, Rickey moved ahead with his plans. He didn't want Robinson to be the only black face on the Montreal roster in 1946. In early February, just as Robinson was returning from Venezuela, Rickey signed 27-year-old pitcher John Wright of the Homestead Grays. According to most accounts, Wright was signed to serve as Robinson's companion. Yet many in the Negro Leagues considered him the better prospect. While he, too, was a military veteran, Wright was a native of New Orleans and accustomed to the South. He and Robinson shared little more than the same skin color.

Rickey didn't stop there. In quick succession he also signed catcher Roy Campanella, pitcher Don Newcombe, and pitcher Roy Partlow to minor league contracts.

Robinson's on-field success would make him the figure he later became, not the fact that he was the first African-American player Rickey signed. Make no mistake, had Robinson failed, and any of the other four succeeded before him, this book would be about that other player. Their backgrounds would be explored, not Robinson's. Their conversations with Branch Rickey would be recorded, not Robinson's. And their struggles would be fully examined. For while Robinson, in retrospect, appears as the perfect man for the situation, Rickey was not so sure. After signing Robinson he moved quickly to sign other black players, hoping one would succeed

and knowing that each would take pressure off the others.

Following Rickey's advice, and presumably his heart, Robinson married Rachel on February 10. The couple left for spring training two weeks later. The careful planning for which Rickey is so often credited in regard to Robinson is nowhere less apparent than in the way Robinson was treated during spring training over the course of his Dodgers career. His rookie season with the Royals was no exception.

While Rickey had no trouble foreseeing many of the difficulties Robinson would face on the field, in regard to the institutionalized racism of the South, he was not so understanding. It was bad enough that the Royals were holding spring training in Florida, but Rickey insisted on scheduling exhibitions in cities where Robinson's presence on the field violated local laws against race mixing. To his credit, Rickey eventually canceled the games entirely rather than play without Robinson or Wright, but his inability to foresee those problems in advance placed Robinson in a difficult situation and increased the pressure on him. Furthermore, Rickey left Robinson and Wright virtually alone off the field. Jackie and Rachel only found a place to stay through the intervention of Wendell Smith, Sam Lacy, and Billy Rowe, a photographer. The men found a local black family willing to rent a room.

The real fight Robinson faced was on the baseball diamond. He had only a few short weeks to prove he belonged. After a convoluted trip with Rachel from California, Robinson arrived in Sanford, Florida, where the Royals were scheduled to hold camp, on March 3. The couple had intended to fly all the way, but were bumped from several flights due to their racial identity. They finally made the last leg of their journey by bus. Wright, traveling by train, preceded Robinson into camp by three days.

Robinson was so disgusted by the experience

and the lack of assistance provided by the Dodgers concerning their accommodations that he threatened to leave the next day, but Wendell Smith talked him out of it. The great experiment would soon commence.

Prior to Robinson's arrival, Rickey read the riot act to all 150 players in camp, warning them that he would not tolerate trouble. He sent a similar message to Montreal Manager Clay Hopper, a native Mississippian, who despite his college degree had a hard time even admitting that African-Americans were human. But Hopper and the other players got the message. They all wanted to make the major leagues, and didn't need Branch Rickey standing in their way. Robinson and Wright had little trouble with their fellow Royals.

The same could not be said of the city of Sanford, Florida, where the Royals were supposed to train. Two days after Robinson's arrival, the Royals had to pull up their stakes and move to Kelly Field in the black section of Daytona Beach. The white residents of Sanford had made it clear that Robinson and Wright were not welcome.

As if this were all not enough for Robinson to face, the Royals already had a shortstop, Sam Breard, a native French-Canadian who was extremely popular in Montreal. In the Royals first inter-squad game on March 7, Robinson started at shortstop, but was soon switched to second.

In the first few weeks of camp, Jackie did little to impress anyone. He proved he could run, but that was all. He had trouble throwing from short, looked awkward at second and failed to hit. Royal pitchers got him out easily on a steady diet of curve balls. Then Robinson came down with a sore arm. Rather than pull him from the Montreal lineup, Rickey ordered that Robinson play first base.

He looked no better there. Fortunately, his arm wasn't permanently injured and he was soon moved back to second, but time was running out. Players were beginning to whisper to one another that Robinson was receiving special treatment. Anyone else performing as poorly would have been cut or sent down.

Robinson was clearly pressing. Rickey did what he could, cajoling Jackie to make use of his speed and giving him pep talks between innings, but there was a limit to his patience. The pressure on Robinson was enormous. He knew it was more important not to fail than it was to succeed. Rickey did not want to admit he was a mistake. Thus far, Johnny Wright had struggled with his control and hadn't looked good either. Jackie failed to get a hit in two games against the Dodgers at the end of the month, but finally began to look comfortable at second and started to make contact against minor league pitching. That's all he had to do. His speed took care of the rest.

The crowds at Royal games that spring were a mixture of the curious, the converted and the cracker. African-American fans usually packed whatever part of the ballpark was designated for their use, while hundreds and sometimes thousands more milled around outside, unable to gain admittance. White fans ranged from the cautiously supportive to the caustic. Some risked attack by cheering lustily for Robinson, some held back and cheered him only when he did something spectacular, while others used his very appearance on the field to vent their malice toward all African-American men.

One group, even then, stood out for their unabashed acceptance of Robinson: children. Young white fans, many of them accompanied by adults who came to hate Robinson, were fascinated by Robinson and took to him immediately. They may have seen him first as a black man, but as soon as Robinson did anything as a player they were caught up in the excitement of the athlete.

Their cheers often emboldened others to join them.

In the Royals final exhibition game, against the Dodgers, Robinson finally came through with the kind of performance Rickey hoped for. The Royals belted the Dodgers, 6-1, the clubs' seventh win in eight games against big league competition, but Robinson banged out two base hits, one each off Eddie Chandler and veteran Art Herring, scored once, stole a base and handled five chances at second base flawlessly. There was no doubt anymore. Robinson and Wright both headed north out of camp with Montreal. They had made the team.

Yet some were not convinced. *The Sporting News* wrote that "There is much doubt whether Jackie Robinson, the Negro second baseman, will hit well enough to hold a regular job." Many noted that the majority of Robinson's spring training hits came on bunts or infield grounders. He had yet to drive the ball.

Jackie Robinson made his debut on April 17 in Jersey City, New Jersey, and any remaining doubts about Robinson's ability were erased in perhaps the best offensive display of his professional career. A standing-room-only crowd of more than twenty-five thousand fans packed Roosevelt Stadium to witness history. Nearly as many roamed the streets outside, for Jersey City Mayor Frank "Boss" Hague declared the day a half-holiday and his minions bullied local businesses into buying tickets.

As a young boy, Editor Ken Hartnett of the *New Bedford Standard-Times* attended the game. He recalls "there was a tremendous amount of anticipation before the game. It was the first season after the war, and everyone was there to see Robinson and all these guys who were coming home." Hartnett remembers that the crowd was "kind of quiet at first, everyone was waiting to see what was going on," but there was still, "an incredible amount of excitement, all focused on Robinson." In the stands, the mostly white crowd kept up a constant murmur about Robinson. He

Jackie Robinson would take a fast track from Montreal to Brooklyn in merely a single season. It is all the more remarkable when one considers that Robinson had played barely one hundred games of organized baseball before joining the Montreal Royals.
(National Baseball Library, Cooperstown, N.Y.)

wasn't peppered with catcalls, "but people were referring to him in the language they used then," words that today would likely cause a riot. Then, remembers Hartnett, "It just built. As the day wore on, he just blew everyone away. At the end of the game, everyone was cheering for him."

Robinson hit second in the Royals lineup, and stepped to the plate with one out in the top of the first against left-handed Jersey City pitcher Warren Sandel. He hit a ground ball to shortstop Jaime Almandre, who threw him out by half a step. The crowd cheered the play like any other.

In the second, the Royals scored two on a home run by right fielder Red Durret to go up 2-0. Robinson stepped to the plate for the second time with Royal pitcher Barney DeForge on second and center fielder Marv Rackley on first.

Sandel delivered, and Robinson turned on the first pitch he saw.

The ball took off on a line to left field and dropped over the fence for a home run.

People in the stands first started to cheer then began to roar as Robinson ran around the bases, too excited to settle into a comfortable jog. Manager Hopper slapped his back as he rounded third. George Shuba met him at home plate, and for the first time in organized baseball a white hand clasped a black one in congratulations. As he reached the dugout Robinson's teammates, realizing the significance of what just happened, swarmed over him. The Royals led, 5-0.

That was just the beginning. Robinson hit again in the fourth. He surprised everyone by dropping a bunt down the third base line, beating third baseman Larry Miggins throw by two steps. The crowd roared.

As relief pitcher Phil Oates toed the rubber and threw home, Robinson broke for second, stealing it easily and again drawing cheers. Then Royals first baseman Tom Tatum hit a hard ground ball to third. Jackie faked returning to second as Miggins fielded the ball, looked

him back, then tossed to first. As soon as the ball left Miggin's hand, Robinson reversed direction and lit out for third, beating the return throw.

With Robinson now only ninety feet from home, Oates pitched from the stretch. Miggins was forced to play the bag like a first baseman, as Robinson pranced farther and farther off base. Oates threw to third three times. Each time, Jackie slid back in safely. The crowd stood on its feet and cheered his safe return.

Once again Robinson faked a dash toward home as Oates toed the rubber. This time the pitcher started toward home, then thought better of it as Robinson began another dash. Oates hesitated in mid-delivery, and the umpire called a balk and waved Robinson home.

This was the play, Hartnett remembers, that really energized the crowd. "Nobody had ever seen anybody run the bases like that before," he says, "You couldn't believe it."

In the seventh, Robinson came to the plate for the fourth time. He singled sharply up the middle, stole second again, moved to third on a base hit by Tatum and scored on Spider Jorgenson's triple to right field.

Yet he wasn't done. In the eighth Jackie dropped another perfect bunt down the third base line for his second bunt hit. Then, with Robinson running on the pitch, Tatum hit another ground ball. The Jersey City infielder, with no chance of catching Jackie at second, threw to first.

As the first baseman received the throw, an alert Robinson rounded second and kept going, beating the startled first baseman's throw to third. By now, the crowd was going nuts. Robinson responded to their growing adulation. He worked more magic, only now Jersey City pitcher Herb Andrew was his victim. For the second time, his bluff down the line caused a balk, and Robinson jogged home with Montreal's thirteenth run.

Jackie was less impressive in the field, although no one was complaining. He threw low to first on a potential double play ball in the fifth for an error, but made up for it in the sixth by starting a neat double play himself, and handled four other chances without incident. Montreal went on to win, 14-1, as Robinson contributed four hits, four RBIs, four runs scored, a home run, two stolen bases and two forced balks. His was a performance out of some kind of epic, an act at once almost unbelievable but at the same time a portend of other miracles yet to be performed.

Hartnett recalls that he felt strangely divided that day. He was thrilled with Robinson's performance, "But I was a fanatical Giants fan as a kid. I lived and breathed guys like Johnny Mize and Bill Voiselle. I wasn't happy to see a great player like Robinson coming up with the Dodgers. And you could tell he was going to be just great."

While Robinson's performance was played down in most mainstream American newspapers, it was not so in the black press or in newspapers north of the border. Baz O'Meara of the *Montreal Star* called Robinson's performance the equivalent "of another Emancipation Day for the Negro Race." In the *Courier*, Wendell Smith covered Robinson's every move from the moment he reached the park. Smith remained on Robinson's trail much of the year, and the *Courier* continued to give Robinson's performance more coverage than that of the Negro Leagues.

Jackie stumbled a bit in his second appearance, making two errors, then another in his third game, but he continued to hit and worry pitchers every time he got on base. Yet it was not his performance on the field that caused him concern. As the Royals made their way through other International League cities, Robinson's reception varied. In Newark, the teams first stop after Jersey City, he received a warm welcome from the fans but a Newark player, outfielder Leon Treadway, reportedly balked at playing against Robinson. He asked for, and received, a demotion.

The problems didn't really begin until the Royals visited Syracuse and Baltimore, the last two stops on their two week long opening road trip. In Syracuse on April 24, an opposing player unleashed a black cat on the field, yelling to Robinson "There's your cousin clowning on the field," and he was on the receiving end of some malicious bench jockeying. A record-breaking weekday crowd of 4,500 turned out in bitter weather to see him play, but unlike the crowds in New Jersey, Syracuse fans rode Robinson mercilessly. For the first time in his brief career, he went hitless.

Baltimore was no better. International League President Frank Shaughnessy warned Rickey not to play Robinson in the southern city, believing it would cause "rioting and bloodshed." Rickey brushed off the warning.

The first game of the series on Saturday, April 27 was a repeat of the experience in Syracuse. On a bitterly cold day, nearly every one of the 3,500 fans in attendance was there to harass Robinson. Nevertheless, Robinson beat out an infield hit, stole a base, and was robbed of a double on a dubious scorer's decision. Johnny Wright turned in his best performance of the young season in relief and the Royals won, 12-7. In the final game of the series, Robinson keyed a 10-0 Montreal win by going 3-for-3 with a double, a stolen base and four runs scored.

The performance did not go unnoticed. He was also hit by a pitch for the first time all year. Baltimore pitcher Paul Calvert came inside and smacked him on the left hand, the first of only two batters Calvert hit of the 342 he faced all year.

Incidents like these were virtually ignored by the press, both black and white. Just as Rickey felt that Jackie Robinson would have to learn to live with such troubles, so did many other whites,

A handshake between Robinson and Rickey in 1947 seals the deal bringing Jackie up to the Dodgers.
(Courtesy Boston Herald)

even those who wanted him to succeed. At the same time, the white press felt that racial incidents had no place in stories about baseball games unless they affected the outcome. Besides, many felt that drawing attention to those such episodes might just spark more. Even Wendell Smith, whose reports boosted sales of the *Courier* by nearly 100,000 copies per week, was mostly silent on the subject. While he played up the smallest instance of goodwill, acts of intolerance were either ignored or referred to obliquely. The black press had already been serving as Robinson's de facto public relation firm for years. Now they honed his image, creating a stalwart hero worthy of being the first African-American in baseball.

The Royals flew from Baltimore to Montreal on April 30, sorely in need of the comforts of home. The club was barely playing .500 baseball and Robinson, although he was hitting over .300, was beginning to feel the pressure. Montreal was a relief, not only for Robinson, but for the black

reporters in his entourage. There, they found a level of acceptance and openness that was impossible in America. Robinson and his wife found a place to stay in a rooming house.

The next day, Montreal celebrated the return of baseball and the debut of Robinson. Sixteen thousand fans packed Delorimier Downs, Montreal's home park, to catch their first glimpse of Robinson, but unfortunately, they didn't see much, as Robinson could manage only one base hit in the 12-9 win over Jersey City. He went hitless on May 2 before being removed from the lineup on May 3 with a sore left hand, a reminder of the pitch thrown by Calvert a few days before.

When Jackie returned to the lineup, he started hitting. Significantly, the Royals started winning. He and Rachel settled into their own apartment and Robinson began to relax in Montreal.

The Montreal fans loved him. Although the city's black population was less than 10,000, the city harbored little racial ill will. Robinson, as a celebrity, was something of a curiosity. He often found friendly crowds of fans waiting for him outside the ballpark; a welcome respite from the reception he received in some other International League cities.

The Royals sent Johnny Wright down to Three Rivers in the Canadian American League on May 14. He hadn't pitched much and had struggled with control when he did. Although Wright and Robinson hadn't been close, the Dodgers organization still felt it was necessary to pair Robinson with another African-American, so they called up pitcher Roy Partlow from Three Rivers. Unlike Wright, Partlow, while talented, was no prospect. Already thirty-six-years-old, he was soon returned to Three Rivers.

The Royals embarked on their second road trip on May 19 and Robinson learned just how fickle baseball fans could be. Although he'd been treated roughly in Syracuse, when the Royals played only a few hundred miles to the west, in Buffalo, he and Partlow were honored by the Buffalo fans and were presented with a wide assortment of gifts. Jackie responded with his best sustained stretch of play of the season, hitting in twelve straight games. During the surge, the Royals took command of first place.

On a return trip to Buffalo in late May, the schizophrenic nature of his unique position was made clear. While Buffalo fans didn't give him trouble, Buffalo players were not so magnanimous. Several times during the series, Bison players rolled into second base, sending Robinson sprawling. The rough play took its toll. As the Royals traveled to Rochester on May 29, Robinson's right leg stiffened and swelled. The team trainer commented with some irony it was "not only black, but blue."

His leg was slow to heal and Robinson missed much of the next three weeks. On several occasions, he tried to play, but after a game or two had to return to the sidelines.

Jackie still appeared on the field, coaching first on several occasions. It was good business but left him exposed to the venom of the fans. Money talked louder than concerns over either Robinson's safety or his psyche. He was the biggest draw in the league. Wherever he played, attendance records fell. In a season when total major-league attendance was just more than nine million, Robinson's Royals drew more than one million fans, over one-third the total for the entire league.

Robinson didn't return to the lineup for good until June 21. By then, the Royals had the International League pennant race well in hand. While few of the Royals would go on to big league careers, and none as successfully as Robinson, they were an experienced and talented group of ballplayers. In the infield, Robinson teamed with shortstop Al Campanis, while Spider Jorgenson played third and Tom Tatum and Lester Burge shared first. In the outfield, fleet-footed Marv Rackley, Irv Naylor, and George Shuba were more than able. Herman Franks and veteran Dixie Howell shared catching duties, while infielder Lew Riggs was an invaluable mid-season pickup. The pitching staff made up for what it lacked in talent with depth and experience.

The Royals played aggressive, hellbent-for-leather baseball. They ran the bases with abandon, stealing 189 for the year, and outscored every other team in the league by more than two hundred runs. Their defense paced the league.

Robinson was a perfect fit. The Royals exploited his talents to the fullest. He ran at will and made use of the foremost of his talent. On another club, Robinson might have been restricted. On the Royals, he was allowed to vent his private frustrations on the field.

And Robinson was frustrated. By August, although he was hitting over .360 and in a battle

*The plaque unveiled in Montreal in 1977 marking the
thirtieth anniversary of Robinson's breaking the color line in
modern Major League Baseball.*
(National Baseball Library, Cooperstown, N.Y.)

for the league batting title, Robinson feared he
was starting to crack.

The pressure he felt was both external and
self-imposed. While he was not always the object
of racial hatred, at every moment Robinson felt as
if he were under a spotlight. He believed he
could not afford to fail or let up for a moment.

The Dodgers did little to help him, on or off
the field. While on the one hand Branch Rickey
Jr. spent several weeks traveling with the club and
pronounced it devoid of prospects, at the same
time *Courier* writer Sam Maltin was reporting
that the Dodgers were on the verge of calling
Jackie up. Robinson also had to deny rumors that
he was going to quit baseball to return to college,

and deal with the pregnancy of Rachel, who was
expecting in December.

Somehow Jackie responded with the best play
of the season. In a five-game stretch against
Syracuse and Jersey City, he went 16-for-23,
pushing his average to .375 and causing the
Montreal press to go apoplectic. Still, Robinson's
stomach was bothering him, and he had periodic
trouble sleeping. He was feeling more than the
mental strain of playing. Physically, he was spent.
Robinson had been playing baseball in three
countries on two continents with three teams,
with only the odd week or two off, for nearly a
year and a half. He was exhausted.

In mid-August, his average started to drop,
which caused him to worry some more. Finally,
in early September, with only a few days left in
the season, he went to a doctor. After a thorough
examination he was pronounced physically fit but
it was suggested he take a few days off. His problems were clearly the result of the combined
effects of stress and exhaustion, exacerbated by
his own worries. He stayed away from the ballpark for two days, then told Clay Hopper he was
fit. Jackie held a slim lead in the league batting
race, and he didn't want anyone to think he
backed into a batting title. He didn't, and finished at .349, a Montreal record, five points ahead
of Newark's Al Clark. He also led the league with
113 runs scored, and his 40 stolen bases trailed
only teammate Marv Rackley.

The Royals finished the regular season at 100-
54, 18 1/2 games ahead of second place Syracuse.
On September 11, the Royals met fourth place
Newark in the semifinals of the International
League playoffs. Paced by Robinson's three hits
and three runs scored, Montreal took game one,
7-5, then dropped two of the next three as
Robinson managed only a single base hit. The
Royals won game five 2-1 to go up in the series
three games to two.

The clincher took place September 18 in

Montreal. Robinson contributed two doubles to the cause but the Royals still trailed, 4-3, with two out in the ninth. First baseman Les Burge appeared to strike out to end the game, but the umpire called the 2-2 pitch a ball. On the next pitch, he tied the score with a home run, leading to a near riot as the Newark bench charged umpire Art Gore to protest the earlier call. Gore threw out Manager George Selkirk and three players before order was restored. Tom Tatum then singled and Herman Franks doubled, sending Tatum home. Gore called Tatum safe on a close play to end the series, and the Bears erupted again. Yogi Berra had to be physically restrained from assaulting the ump. The police and Montreal players escorted Gore from the field to prevent the Bears from attacking him.

The win sent the Royals up against Syracuse in the finals. It was another raucous series. After losing the opener, Montreal whipped Syracuse in four straight. The series was marred by a vicious bean ball war that cost Montreal the services of catcher Herman Franks after he was struck in the head in the series final game. But the win earned Montreal the right to play the Louisville Colonels, the American Association champions, in the Little World Series.

Robinson was the focus from the very beginning. No African-American had appeared on a baseball field in Louisville with whites before, and the city was not in an accepting mood. On the eve of the series, thousands of white citizens had taken to the streets to protest the admission of blacks into a local hospital.

The series opened September 28. Thirteen thousand fans packed tiny Parkway Field to capacity, most with the express purpose of making Jackie Robinson's life miserable. Only a small area was set aside for black fans, for when it became clear the Royals would be the Colonels' opponents, Louisville team officials announced that all tickets would be sold on a reserved basis.

During warmups the crowd kept up a steady string of boos and racial cat calls whenever Robinson touched the ball. That was only the beginning. Jackie was the second batter in the first inning. As soon as he emerged from the dugout, the boos began again.

Outside the park, thousands of black fans milled around, unable to gain admittance. They climbed fences and scaled rooftops in an effort to see their hero.

The Royals won, 7-5, as Les Burge cracked out two home runs. But Robinson went hitless.

To be fair, not everyone in Louisville was looking for Robinson to fail. Baseball writer Tommy Fitzgerald of the *Louisville Courier Journal* was sympathetic to Robinson in his coverage of the series, commenting after game one that Robinson took the crowd's venom "most gracefully and conducted himself in his every move as a gentleman." The presence of Louisville native Dixie Howell behind the plate for the Royals may have helped keep some fans at bay, and by in large the Louisville players left Robinson alone. Still, the treatment from the crowd was among the worst he had faced all season.

Game two was delayed nearly a half an hour when the Louisville players refused to take the field. Although some have argued that Robinson was the cause of the delay, that perception is incorrect. In game one, Colonel Manager Nemo Leibold, who had earlier been suspended for 45 days for assaulting an umpire, had to restrain Louisville catcher Fred Walters after a disputed call. Before game two, Walters was called on the carpet by the three man commission running the series. Leibold, offended at Walters treatment, was ordered to meet with the commission himself, but stalked out of the meeting and was also suspended.

When the Louisville players found out, they refused to play. Faced with an impatient mob in the stands, the commission rescinded the suspen-

Brooklyn Manager Leo Durocher and Robinson during spring training in 1947. (Associated Press, National Baseball Library, Cooperstown, N.Y.)

sion. Still, the Royals took the field unclear about what had just transpired. Robinson was clearly distracted and he went hitless again as Louisville tied the series on a 3-0 shutout by Harry Dorish. The crowd was even more vociferous in their disapproval of Robinson than in game one, as many in the stands erroneously thought he was somehow the reason for the delay.

Branch Rickey himself traveled to Louisville for game three. Robinson scored two runs, but the Colonels routed six Royals pitchers, cracking out nineteen hits and winning 15-6. The Royals returned to Montreal down two games to one.

Robinson's treatment by the Louisville fans went virtually unreported everywhere but in Montreal. There, the sports writers who followed the club let Royals fans know precisely what Robinson had been facing. When the Royals took the field for game four of the series, the crowd let them know how they felt.

Each time Robinson took the field, stood at the plate or touched the ball, Montreal fans stood and roared. And each time a Louisville player was introduced, they reacted with a chorus of boos. Nevertheless, the Colonels took a quick 4-0 lead before the Royals started scratching back. In the ninth, with the Colonels still leading 5-3, Louisville pitcher Otie Clark came unglued.

On April 10, 1947 Jackie Robinson entered Ebbets Field in a Royals uniform and left as a member of the Brooklyn Dodgers.
(Associated Press, National Baseball Library, Cooperstown, N.Y.)

As the Montreal fans roared and hooted, Clark walked the bases full with two outs. Reliever Joe Ostrowski came in and walked in a run to make the score 5-4. Robinson was on second and trotted to third, while Tom Tatum went from first to second. But Colonels catcher Fred Walters got cute. He tried to catch Tatum napping and threw to second.

The throw went wide and Robinson scored to tie the game 5-5.

Then the Colonels stiffened. The game went into extra innings. Louisville failed to score in the top half, but the Royals loaded the bases in the bottom of the inning. Robinson stepped to the plate with 13,000 voices cheering his name. He responded by spanking the ball into left field for a single, giving the Royals a 6-5 win and knotting the series.

Now Jackie was back in his game. In game five, he smacked a seventh-inning triple and later scored to put the Royals up 4-3, then secured the victory in the ninth by beating out a squeeze bunt to knock in Al Campanis from third. The *Courier Journal* summed up the game nicely, running a headline over the box score that read simply "Robinson."

The Colonels couldn't stop the Royals in game six. Curt Davis spun a shutout and Dixie Howell's two-run homer in the second inning provided all the runs Montreal required. Robinson had two hits and contributed several nifty fielding plays to the cause. He did not, however, score the winning run, for which he mistakenly takes credit in his autobiography *I Never Had It Made*.

The scene after the game was something out of a movie. Thousands of Montreal fans rushed the field, singing "Il a gagne ses Epaulettes [He won his bars, or spurs]," and chanting in English, "We want Robinson." The Royals retreated to the clubhouse, but first Clay Hopper, then Curt Davis, returned to the field. They were lifted to the shoulders of admiring fans and carried around the field.

Still, the crowd refused to leave. They wanted Robinson.

Ushers were dispatched to the clubhouse to retrieve him. When Jackie emerged from the dugout, he was lost in a swarm of men, women, and children who attacked him with joy.

When he finally made his way back to the clubhouse, the crowd left the field and waited outside. Ushers and police tried without success to make a path for his escape, but failed. Finally, Robinson put his head down and tried to push his way through the crowd, meeting with resistance stiffer but far more loving than any he had ever faced on the football field.

He finally broke away and ran down the street with the joyous mob in hot pursuit. He traveled three blocks before a stranger pulled up in a car and motioned for him to jump in. He did without thinking and landed on a woman's lap. They delivered him safely to his hotel.

Sam Maltin of the *Pittsburgh Courier* penned the definitive account of the scene. Of Robinson he wrote, "He's strictly Brooklyn. He never belonged in this league, despite his Class AAA rating after the first month of play." Maltin ended his story eloquently. "To the large group of Louisville fans who came here with their team, it may be a lesson of goodwill among men. That it's the man and not his color, race, or creed. They couldn't fail to tell others down South of the riots, the chasing of a Negro—not because of hate, but because of love."

Robinson's run would soon land him in Brooklyn.

History's Man

By David Halberstam

He was history's man. Nothing less. Though he came to the nation disguised as a mere baseball player, he was, arguably, the single most important American of that first post war decade. It was not just that he was the first black to play our one showcased national sport, nor that he did it with so dazzling a combination of fire and ice, that he was in truth the black Cobb. What made him so important was the particular moment when he arrived and the fact that he stood at the exact intersection of two powerful and completely contradictory American impulses, one the impulse of darkness and prejudice, the other the impulse of idealism and optimism, the belief in the possibility of true advancement for all Americans in this democratic and meritocratic society.

It is easy now, a half century after Jackie Robinson first played for the Dodgers, when we live in an age of Michael Jordan and Scottie Pippen, and Jerry Rice and Emmitt Smith and Frank Thomas and Bobby Bonds and countless other brilliant black athletes to forget the ethos which existed in America of the 1940s, just before Robinson broke in with the Dodgers. There was a special cruelty to it: for this society not only blocked black athletes from competing on a level playing field, and it did not merely prevent them from gaining their rightful and just rewards from their God given athletic talents. We as a country were worse than that: we discriminated against blacks, prevented them from playing, and having done that, we denigrated them and said that the reason that they could not play in our great arenas with our best whites athletes, was because they were not good enough.

We defied elemental fairness. We denied them entry to our greatest and most revered arenas, and having done that, we said that the fault was theirs, that they, the they being Negroes (though that was not the word which was used, of course) did not deserve to play with our great whites because they were not good enough. They were, we said, too lazy. We also said of them that they were gutless, and would not in critical situations show the requisite grittiness and toughness demanded of big league ball players. And having said both those things, and having denied almost all blacks in the country any kind of parity of education in those years, we also said that they were not smart enough to play our big time sports. The only thing they could do—this was self evident from track meets—was run fast. The issue of courage was particularly pernicious: even if they seemed to have enough natural talent, we said, they would fold under the pressure of big games. Having said this, and it was, I assure you, passed on as a kind of folk gospel at the bar of a thousand saloons, and on the sandlots of a thousand small towns and cities, we denied them any chance to give the lie to words so uniquely ugly, and indeed un-American. Their athletic bell curve, was so to speak, not as good as ours. This, by the way, was not just said in the South, where the reasons for blocking any progress by black people was obvious; rather it was said all over the country. That was one part of the ethos of the time.

The other completely contradictory impulse was that of elemental American fairness. It is critical to our national sense of self identity that we believe that we are above all, a fair and just society where every child has as much right to prosper as any other child. The greatest and most obvious arena where this could be proved was, of course, sports. We had as a nation always thought of sports as a place where American democracy proved its own validity and where generation after generation of new immigrants showed their worthiness as Americans by prospering first here before they went on to excel in other fields. We as a nation had, for example, on the eve of World War II, taken special pride in the success of the DiMaggio family of San Francisco, that the three children of the immigrant fishermen had made it to the big leagues, and that one of them, Joseph, was the greatest player of his era. That proved that American democracy worked. There was, sadly, only one ethnic group excluded from that exclusionary vision right up until 1947.

Therefore Jackie Robinson's timing in 1947 was impeccable. It was the perfect moment to create a broader, more inclusive definition of American democracy. For it took place right after the victory over Nazi Germany and authoritarian Japan in a great war which was viewed in this country because of the intensity of our domestic propaganda, as nothing less than a victory of democracies over totalitarian states, of good over evil. It had been a war about elemental justice. A generation of young Americans who had gone off to fight in that war returned more determined than ever to make this country whole in terms of justice and fairness. The kind of discrimination which had been practiced against native born black Americans up until then was no longer feasible. At stake was the most elementary American concept of fairness, in this most democratic of venues, sports. In American folk mythology, a rich kid who had a fancy uniform and an expensive glove still had to prove, when he tried out for a team, that he was a better player than some poor kid from the wrong side of town who did not even own a glove. Now that basic concept of fairness was about to be applied along a racial divide as it never had been before.

It was the conflict between these two conflicting concepts of which Jackie Robinson became the sole arbiter. To most citizens of the country, particularly younger Americans, anxious that their country be as fair and just as it claimed it was, Robinson's debut was more than an athletic performance; rather it was like a political work in progress, an ongoing exercise in the possibilities of American democracy. When he finally arrived in this most open and public of arenas, not only was the whole country watching, but Robinson was performing in an area where success was stunningly easy to calibrate—every school boy could if he wanted, measure the ability of this man. Nothing could be hidden. We are not talking about some great medical school accepting one black student covertly and the rest of the country thereupon not being able to chart that student's progress. Rather we are talking about the perfect arena for so great an experiment. Rarely therefore has one good man given the lie to so much historic ugliness. Branch Rickey had picked well: Robinson was not just a gifted athlete, he was a gifted human being, proud, strong, disciplined, courageous. Robinson did not merely integrate baseball, he did not merely show that blacks could play baseball, and football and basketball as well as whites could, he helped put the end to arguments in other fields. When the Supreme Court ruled on Brown seven years later, and when Martin Luther King came along in Montgomery eight years later, (and when Lt. Colin Luther Powell entered the United States Army eleven years later) the deed was essentially already done. Most of the country was ready in no small part to give blacks a chance in other venues, because Robinson and those who had come immediately after him, like Mays and Aaron had shown in the most final and compelling way, that if blacks were given an equal opportunity, they were more than worthy of it. The argument was over. One vision of America, a cruel and self evidently crippling one, had mercifully come to an end in 1947, and another, infinitely more optimistic, had been greatly strengthened.

David Halberstam is the author of thirteen books including his highly praised triology on power in America: The Best and the Brightest, The Powers That Be and The Reckoning. His first baseball book, Summer of '49, was the number one New York Times hardcover bestseller. He has also written about sports such as basketball and Olympic Rowing. His most recent book is October 1964. He has won every major journalistic award including the Pulitzer Prize. He lives in New York City.

THE FIRST MAN: 1946-1947

Branch Rickey's desire to promote Jackie Robinson to the Dodgers in 1947 was the worst kept secret in baseball. Although Rickey believed Robinson was ready, he was not so sure whether the Dodger organization, organized baseball or the rest of America was quite so prepared. Nevertheless, throughout the fall and winter of 1946, Rickey moved closer to the inevitable.

Rickey did not want a repeat of Robinson's 1946 spring training experience. With the promotion of Robinson to the Dodgers imminent, he moved to alleviate that problem. In mid-September, as Robinson and the Royals were still engaged in the post-season playoffs, Rickey traveled to California and scouted potential spring training sites in Santa Barbara, Santa Ana and Anaheim. Even *The Sporting News* saw through the junket, pronouncing "the cause of the pro-posed switch is believed to be the graduation to the parent club of Jackie Robinson . . . [who is] sure to come up with Brooklyn next season." Branch came away from his trip dissatisfied with either the accommodations, the racial climate, or both, in California. So in October he sent Dodgers Traveling Secretary Harold Parrot to Cuba with Coach Charley Dressen's barnstorming squad to scout sites there.

Rickey liked what Parrot found. Blacks had been playing on integrated teams in Cuba for decades, so it was unlikely that Robinson would face any overt prejudice from the Cuban people. Likewise, Rickey hoped that living in Cuba and playing exhibitions against local teams would calm any Dodgers fears about playing with a black man while providing a quick lesson in the advantages of integration.

Just after the World Series he announced that

the Dodgers would train in Cuba in 1947. Yet the potential promotion of Robinson was only part of his decision. The threat posed by the Mexican League in 1946 had alerted Major League Baseball to the importance of Latin America. Organized baseball recognized the need to increase its presence in Latin America in order to subvert the development of similar "outlaw" leagues. Rickey's decision to have the Dodgers train in Havana fit nicely with the larger plans of Major League Baseball. Within a year, baseball would act to bring Cuba under the umbrella of the National Association, cutting off a potential source of competition.

With the location of spring training decided, Rickey's next challenge was to find a position for Robinson to play on the Dodgers. Shortstop was out. Pee Wee Reese was a star and the Dodgers had already decided that Robinson's arm wasn't strong enough to play the position. While Robinson had proven himself at second base, he was likewise shut out at that position. Eddie Stanky, whom the Dodgers had previously thought of as merely a good wartime player, was a pleasant surprise in 1946 and had a firm grip on the spot. Besides, he was one of Durocher's favorites. Robinson was a man without a position.

The return of players from military service in 1947 made matters more complicated. So much experienced talent was pouring out of the military that active rosters were expanded in order to give returning servicemen the best possible chance to regain their old spots. Younger players who gained experience during the war years had to prove themselves all over again. Any position not manned by an established star was up for grabs. This situation worked both for and against Robinson. Although it gave the Dodgers a chance to experiment, it also increased the competition Robinson would encounter trying to make the team.

Rickey used Leo Durocher to float trial balloons in the press so he could measure public reaction. As much as possible, Rickey wanted the focus to be on Robinson's ability as a player. Speaking to reporters in Hollywood in mid-November, Durocher stated that "Potentially, he [Robinson] is one of the best third basemen in the game." That was strong language about a player who had never before played that position. Durocher went on to say "He's a great bunter and pivot man on double plays . . . [and] one of the finest gentlemen on the Montreal club and we'll be glad to have him with us on the Dodgers, providing he shows he's ready for the big leagues." Durocher also intimated that the Dodgers were looking into signing Kenny Washington, Robinson's old UCLA football teammate. Clearly, Rickey was moving ahead.

A few days later Rickey reiterated Durocher's comments. "We're six deep at third base," he told reporters, "Tom Brown may be out of the Army. We have in addition, Miksis, Jorgenson, Mauch, Tatum—and Jackie Robinson." In another curious move, he also announced plans to offer all seats at Ebbets Field on a reserved basis. He claimed this decision was for the convenience of fans, but it also allowed Rickey to gauge how well Brooklyn fans would accept an African-American player before he actually appeared on the field.

At the same time, it became increasingly clear to the men who owned baseball that breaking the color line might just be good business. In October, Bob Feller's barnstorming squad of major leaguers played an eighteen game schedule throughout the Midwest and West against Satchel Paige's team of Negro League stars. Feller's club went 13-5, but the series drew more than 250,000 rabid fans who didn't care what color the players were, making it the most lucrative such tour to date. Baseball owners were shocked later that winter to learn that many players on Feller's team actually earned more during their short season

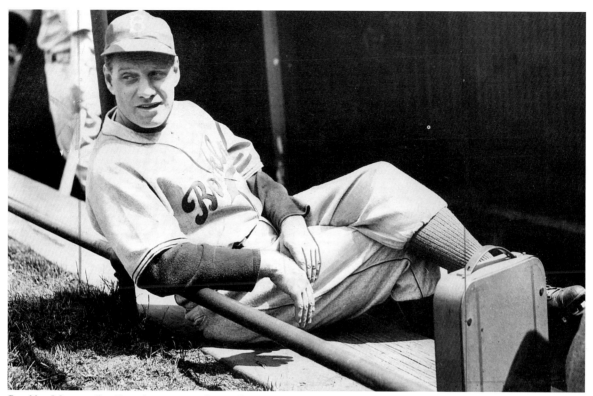

Brooklyn Manager Leo Durocher never made it to Opening Day in 1947 as he was suspended by Commisioner Chandler on April 9 for one season. (Courtesy of The Boston Herald)

than they did during the regular season. Clearly, there was money to be made from integrated baseball.

In the off-season Robinson had played with Chet Brewer's all-black Kansas City Royals. Jackie was the main attraction. Fans saw a ballplayer much different from the one who played the season before in Montreal. Unfettered by Rickey's strictures on his behavior, Robinson vented some of his frustrations.

In an October 25 game against Feller's squad in Los Angeles, the only meeting between the two teams of the winter season, Robinson halted play on three separate occasions as he argued ball and strike calls with the home plate umpire. With Leo Durocher looking on from the stands, Robinson stepped from the on deck circle and argued with plate umpire Gordon Ford. Robinson then took his at-bat and continued the

argument when Ford called a strike. Later in the game, as he stood on second base, Robinson berated Gordon a third time, leading Halley Hardy, sports editor of the black *Los Angeles Tribune*, to take him to task. Halley called Robinson's outbursts, "uncalled for," and asserted they "did him no good," adding "Jackie has a lot to learn if that is a sample of the way he expects to conduct himself in Major League Baseball."

Although the tour drew sizable crowds, the promoters stole the proceeds. Robinson ended up laying out several thousand dollars of his own money to pay off his teammates.

Still, the tour stimulated interest in Robinson across the nation. Fans everywhere were curious about Robinson and the talent of black players in general. When the barnstorming season ended in November, Bob Feller was quizzed by writers about his impressions of the opposition.

While Feller acknowledged that, "Some are good hitters. Some can field pretty good. [And] Most of them are fast," he added, "I have seen none that combine the qualities of a big league ballplayer." Perhaps Paige, he grudgingly admitted, could have played in the majors, "when he was young."

When a reporter asked, "Not even Jackie Robinson?" Feller was adamant, responding, "Not even Jackie Robinson." Indeed, in the earlier game against Robinson's team, Feller struck Jackie out three times. Feller later commented that Robinson's bat was slow, a factor he attributed to his "football shoulders."

None of this affected Rickey's plans. As fall turned into winter, he fretted over the design and implementation of a complicated strategy to bring Robinson into the big leagues. In its final form, Robinson would receive a more-than-fair shot and leave Rickey in a position to take credit for his success. Yet at the same time, the strategy was designed to get Rickey off the hook if Robinson failed.

Rickey saw potential obstacles everywhere, not the least of which was the response of the men who owned baseball. In early January, the owners convened a secret meeting at the Waldorf-Astoria hotel in New York to discuss the race question. No minutes were kept of the meeting, and what went on there is dependent on the recollections of baseball Commissioner Happy Chandler. According to Chandler, Rickey told the other owners he planned to promote Robinson. To a man, the other fifteen men who owned baseball teams stood up and announced their opposition. When Rickey's arguments failed to change any minds, he introduced a resolution of support, hoping that some owners, under the protection of a secret ballot, might give him their blessing.

Many have speculated that Baseball Commissioner Happy Chandler, shown here with Joseph P. Kennedy at Braves Field in 1948, supported Robinson in part as the result of his political aspirations that would later include an aborted run for President.
(Courtesy of The Boston Herald)

The vote remained fifteen to one against Rickey's resolution. He stormed from the room.

Yet hope was not lost. Had Judge Landis still been commissioner, he never would have allowed the question to be raised in the first place. Happy Chandler was different. He acted as a moderator at the meeting and kept his own views to himself. A few days later, Rickey paid a visit to the commissioner at his expansive log cabin in Versailles, Kentucky. Rickey pleaded his case to Chandler alone. He made full use of his estimable powers of persuasion, one moment arguing that bringing up Robinson was the moral thing to do, then at the next moment claiming that if he didn't bring Robinson up, there would surely be race riots the following spring. He begged for Chandler's support.

According to Chandler's account of the meeting—which Rickey never admitted took place—the commissioner listened patiently. When Rickey finally stopped talking, Chandler responded by citing the sacrifice that black soldiers made during the war and said "I'm going to have to meet my Maker some day and if he asks me why I didn't let this boy play and I say it's because he's black that might not be a satisfactory answer. So bring him in. Transfer Robinson. And we'll make the fight. There's going to be trouble."

What Chandler meant was that when Rickey eventually sent Robinson's contract to the Commissioner's office for approval, as all baseball contracts had to be, Chandler would approve it. The opposition of the other owners didn't matter. His was an administrative decision.

Not that the other owners couldn't still take action. They could. But they would have to do so publicly, for the color line was merely a gentleman's agreement. Even in 1947, making such a secret agreement public policy would have placed baseball at legal odds with burgeoning fair employment regulations.

Rickey's end run worked, whether he expected it to or not. The other owners, and perhaps even Rickey, had never dreamt that Chandler would go against their wishes. But Chandler was thinking beyond baseball: just as Rickey was motivated by the bottom line, Chandler was motivated by his political prospects. The commissioner still considered his future to be in politics. He even dreamed of running for president, and was astute enough to know that his reaction to Rickey's proposal would surely have political ramifications. The question of segregation, particularly for a Kentucky politician, demanded a delicate response. Landing too hard on either side of the issue risked loss of support from the other end. A moderate course was called for.

Chandler's tacit approval was the prudent, politically savvy decision. In effect, Chandler ruled in the manner of the U.S. Supreme Court, which can either choose to rule on a particular issue or choose not to and leave decisions to lesser courts. As baseball commissioner, Chandler was directed to enforce the laws of the game. Those laws stated simply that a player need only be under a valid contract. Race was not mentioned. Legally, Rickey could sign whomever he wanted. Chandler simply concluded he did not have the authority to rule on the question. Publicly, Chandler chose neither to support nor criticize Rickey's move, the wisdom of which would eventually be decided by the American people.

Chandler's strategy assured that he would land on the winning side. If Robinson succeeded and the integration of baseball was accepted, no one could later accuse Chandler of standing in the way. If Robinson failed or baseball was torn apart by the issue, Chandler, who served at the behest of the owners, could quietly allow himself to be directed by them or find a reason to step aside. Rickey would stand alone. The secret nature of the meeting itself gave Chandler the freedom to not step in.

One must keep in mind that Chandler's account of these events did not surface for some thirty-five years, and the revelations played a huge role in his eventual selection to the Baseball Hall of Fame. Rickey's own papers, which are suspiciously incomplete about anything concerning Robinson, reportedly say nothing about the meeting. According to Chandler's account, the Robinson question was all the two men talked about. But a close examination of other issues that concerned both men at the time make that unlikely and leave more questions than answers.

Rickey and Chandler had other pressing issues in common. Rickey's decision to hold spring training in Cuba clearly served the interests of the other owners and may have been made to give him some bargaining power. Then there is the curious question of Leo Durocher.

The flamboyant manager was at loggerheads with Chandler. Earlier that winter, Durocher had claimed that Lee MacPhail of the Yankees had offered to make him New York's manager. At the same time, Durocher was carrying on a very public love affair with actress Larraine Day, and charges surfaced that he was consorting with gamblers. This started a war of words between MacPhail, Durocher and the Dodgers that would escalate all spring long before coming to a head at the precise moment Rickey made the official decision to promote Robinson. The timing of the two events could not appear more suspect.

For the moment, the outcome of the meeting with Chandler allowed Rickey to move ahead, and in early February he called a meeting with about three-dozen black leaders at the Brooklyn YMCA.

Although Rickey had all but decided to call up Robinson, the purpose of the meeting was to warn the black leaders to stay in their place. He didn't want anyone to politic for Robinson's promotion. Then, in the event he was promoted, Rickey cautioned the leaders to control their constituency.

In a thundering speech, Rickey warned "the biggest threat to his success, the one enemy most likely to ruin that success, is the Negro people themselves . . . On the day Robinson enters the big leagues—if he does—we don't want any Negro to add to the burden of Jackie Robinson. We don't want any Negroes to form gala welcoming committees, to form parades to the ballpark every night. We don't want Negroes to strut, to wear badges . . . We don't want Negroes in the stands gambling, drunk, fighting, being arrested."

He went on, concluding "If any individual, group or segment of Negro society uses the advancement of Jackie Robinson as a triumph of race over race, I will regret the day I ever signed him and I will personally see that baseball is never so abused and misrepresented again."

The meeting is revealing, not simply for the content of Rickey's speech, but for the fact that he felt the meeting necessary in the first place. It provides strong evidence that while Rickey believed the time was right for baseball to break the color bar, even he was still operating under a disquieting set of racial presumptions and distrust.

Rickey's own racial attitudes were still piously paternalistic. He still viewed Robinson and every other African-American as children in need of instruction. Just as Rickey feared Robinson's explosiveness, so too did he fear the explosiveness of all African-Americans. He was not convinced black crowds would be able to control their emotions. He ignored the fact that every winter thousands and thousands of blacks attended barnstorming exhibitions between teams of blacks and whites virtually without incident; that blacks and whites had played and competed together on the semi-pro, collegiate and prep level in many Northern, Midwestern and Western cities for years; and that mixed crowds had been attending pro boxing matches between blacks and whites for decades.

Leo Durocher with wife, actress Larraine Day, watch the Dodgers train in Havana Cuba in March 1947. (Courtesy of The Boston Herald)

Rickey's admonitions suggest he still divided African-Americans into "good" blacks, who were basically subservient and knew how to act in the white world, and "bad" blacks, who indulged in baser behavior and needed to be controlled. Only the black leaders, acting under Rickey's instructions, could control the races' passions.

He had already exerted such control over Robinson himself. In the off-season, Jackie had been scheduled to be a speaker for a series of fund-raisers for the Detroit Committee to Fight Racial Injustice and Terrorism, only to abruptly cancel without explanation. There is little doubt that Rickey was behind the withdrawal. Robinson was "his," and was to take part only in Rickey's immediate cause: the integration of the Brooklyn Dodgers. Other activities that even hinted of a larger political agenda were off limits.

For the black leaders in attendance, the greater good—the integration of baseball—was impor-

tant enough that they accepted Rickey's stern admonition. While many in the crowd were privately offended, they adopted the slogan "Don't Spoil Jackie's Chances," and promised the cooperation of the black community.

To be fair, most African-American political causes were subjected to being smeared with the taint of communism, a dangerous tag to wear in that inflammatory age. Rickey surely wanted to avoid the perception that either he or Robinson was a dupe of the communists. But that particular paranoia also coincided neatly with Rickey's own, long-established perceptions of racial stereotypes, and likely was not his primary motivation in calling the meeting.

But despite all his careful planning, Rickey was blind to his own insensitivities, and his treatment of Robinson during spring training in Cuba nearly botched everything. The Dodgers forty-seven day stay in Havana has long been regarded as the culmination of Rickey's careful planning in regard to Robinson's eventual call-up. In fact, nothing could be further from the truth. Dodgers camp that spring was a disaster in every way possible. If Rickey had any secret plan concerning the way he wanted to bring Robinson up to the big leagues, it was extraordinarily naive and inept.

Spring training began in late February with the Dodgers becoming perhaps the first team in history to hold camps simultaneously in three countries, on two continents, in two hemispheres.

The Dodgers and AAA Royals trained in Cuba, with extended excursions to Panama and Venezuela. The remaining Dodgers minor leaguers trained in Pensacola, Florida.

This arrangement was awkward from the beginning, as Rickey and other Dodgers officials spent half of spring training shuttling back and forth between the sites. The decision to train the Dodgers and Royals apart in Cuba was supposedly made for Robinson's benefit. In Cuba, Jackie wouldn't face the racism he faced in Florida the previous spring. Besides, Rickey hoped the other Dodgers would grow accustomed to being around blacks in a multiracial country.

It may have been a fine plan, but Rickey nearly ruined it by inadvertently enforcing his own racial attitudes. The Dodgers players stayed at the grand Hotel Nacional, a four-star facility of Moorish design in the heart of Havana. Accommodations were plush, and food was sumptuous. The team trained at Gran Stadium, which was only a few years old. The Royals, on the other hand, held camp at the National Military Academy, a private school for the children of Cuba's elite. While hardly the Hotel Nacional, the academy barracks were more than sufficient, and while the food lacked the elan of the Hotel Nacional, it was still fresh and plentiful.

But four Royals stayed elsewhere. Jackie Robinson and three other African-Americans on the Royal roster—Don Newcombe, Roy Partlow, and Roy Campanella—were put up at the Hotel Boston, a seedy fleabag some fifteen miles away. The four men were given a car and food allowance and left to fend for themselves. Campanella knew a few Spanish words. The others knew none.

Robinson was shocked at the filthy conditions in the hotel, and at first blamed Cuban officials. Then he learned Rickey was behind the slight. Despite the fact the Hotel Nacional was integrated, Rickey told Robinson he feared that the slightest racial incident would undermine his plans. He felt it was best to keep the four black players apart from the other players, yet he took virtually no precautions concerning the quality of their lodgings. Robinson neither agreed nor understood Rickey's reasoning, but nevertheless accepted his explanation. The Mahatma apparently had no idea that he was making an already difficult situation even more difficult for Robinson.

Jackie's relationship with Rickey was complicated. For despite the thousand slights Rickey subjected him to time and time again over the course of his career, Robinson never blamed Rickey for anything, and considered him something of a father figure. He gave Rickey the benefit of the doubt on racial matters, reasoning that Rickey was ultimately responsible for the most significant event of his life: reaching the big leagues. In Robinson's mind, that forgave lesser slights. In spite of evidence otherwise, he either failed to see, or refused to acknowledge publicly, that Rickey was ever less than perfect or ever acted with less than Robinson's own best interests in mind.

The curious arrangements in Cuba did have one desired effect: holding so many separate camps kept the press at bay. Only a few New York newspapers even bothered sending reporters to Cuba to cover the camps. Most relied on wire reports. This enabled the Dodgers to control the press and have Robinson train in virtual seclusion. It also allowed Rickey to put another of his "plans" into effect.

Thus far, Rickey had encouraged speculation that Robinson might play third base. But Arky Vaughan, a former all-star shortstop for Pittsburgh who played infield for the Dodgers in 1942 and 1943 before voluntarily retiring and entering the service, had returned. On the plane to Havana, Wendell Smith buttonholed Durocher and quizzed him about the club. While Durocher had nothing but praise for Robinson, calling him "a damn good ballplayer," and "my type of player," he also intimated that he considered Vaughn his third baseman. On March 2 in Havana, he told Ross McGowan of the *New York Times* the same thing, lauding the returned star and all but giving him the third base spot.

Yet several weeks before, another plan sur-

faced. Rickey had again used Wendell Smith to float an idea, telling him "the weakest spot on the Brooklyn roster is first base."

It was a curious statement. Earlier, he had expressed satisfaction with the platoon of Ed Stevens and Howie Schultz at first. In 1946, Stevens, a lefthander, had accounted for 10 home runs and 60 RBIs, second best on the club to Pete Reiser, while the right-handed Schultz stood six-foot-six and provided a huge target at first. Together, they had combined for 87 RBIs and an impressive 48 extra base hits the previous season. Moreover, Stevens was only twenty-one years-old, Schultz twenty-three. Both seemed likely to improve.

In early April, Arthur Daley of the *Times* intimated that something important could happen soon. "Durocher doesn't know," Daley wrote, "but there is a development in the wind that is

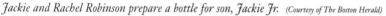

Jackie and Rachel Robinson prepare a bottle for son, Jackie Jr. (Courtesy of The Boston Herald)

Dodgers coach Frenchy Bordargaray (left) with first baseman Howie Schultz. Schultz also gave way to Robinson for the first base job in 1947. (National Baseball Library, Cooperstown, N.Y.)

surprising. Beyond that hint this reporter isn't permitted to say. When it comes, it will knock your hat off."

In fact, it was already in the works. In the off-season, Schultz played professional basketball for the Anderson (Indiana) Duffey Packers of the National Basketball League. With Rickey's permission, he was a late arrival at spring training. In a recent interview, Schultz recalled, "When I got on the plane to Havana, Clyde Sukeforth was on the plane, and he gave me an indication of what was going to happen. Sukeforth gave me an indication that Robinson was going to play first."

When Schultz arrived in Havana, the Dodgers were in Caracas, Venezuela playing an exhibition slate with the Yankees. Instead of sending him to join his teammates, Sukeforth sent Schultz to the Royals camp. When he arrived, according to Schultz, "Sukeforth asked me if I would mind working out with Robinson at first base."

Schultz immediately realized what was happening, and was probably the first Dodgers player to learn that Rickey planned to use Robinson at first base. It could have been an awkward situation, but Schultz was surprisingly understanding. A native of St. Paul, Minnesota, he had grown up around blacks and says, "I didn't have the same feeling toward Robinson some of the other players did." While he realized that the move might cost him his position, he recognized immediately that "Robinson was such a great athlete," and that the Dodgers were probably correct in making the move. Besides, he was already thinking that his future lay in pro basketball. To his everlasting credit, Schultz could have complained or resisted helping Robinson. He did not, and admits to feeling little awkwardness about the situation. "If nothing else," he remembers, "Jackie might have felt awkward having me there."

It was mid-March before word surfaced in the mainstream press that Robinson was playing first for the Royals—Schultz' role was still a secret—

Dodgers first baseman Ed Stevens (left), shown here with pitcher Les Webber, tutored Robinson on the finer points of first base play and conceded his starting position to the rookie at the urging of Branch Rickey.

(Courtesy of The Boston Herald)

and Ross McGowan openly wondered about Jackie's whereabouts. So far, Robinson had trained virtually in secret. The Dodgers and Royals had not yet played each other and no Dodgers writers had bothered covering the Royals camp. Even Leo Durocher had yet to see Robinson in person.

That didn't mean there wasn't interest in Robinson. The Mexican League, looking for publicity, dangled a $10,000 contract before Robinson. He refused, but may have known that if he failed, or if Rickey failed to promote him, Mexico was still an option.

Once again, Rickey had a plan. On March 17, the Dodgers and Royals were scheduled to play each other in a two-game series in Panama, where the Dodgers had already spent over a week roughing up service clubs and assorted Panamanian all-star teams, including several that included Negro League stars like pitcher Pat Scantlebury. Rickey hoped that once Durocher

saw Robinson perform, he would pester Rickey to add him to the Dodgers roster.

Rickey's plans fell through. Since the beginning of camp, the verbal war between Yankees President Larry MacPhail and the Dodgers had escalated. Chandler had recently admonished Durocher for allowing gambling in the clubhouse, leading Rickey to complain publicly that several gamblers had attended the recent Yankees-Dodgers series in Havana as MacPhail's guests. A column by Durocher in the *Brooklyn Eagle*, "Leo Says," ghost-written by Dodger traveling secretary Harold Parrott, repeated the charges.

MacPhail was incensed, and announced plans to file a formal charge with the Commissioner that Durocher was indulging in "conduct detrimental to baseball." At the same time, Larraine Day's estranged husband charged Durocher with stealing his wife, pushing Durocher from the sports page to the scandal sheets. In response,

Dixie Walker was one of several Dodgers who resented Robinson's presence in the Brooklyn clubhouse. Rickey would soon trade Walker to the Pirates. (National Baseball Library, Cooperstown, N.Y.)

the Catholic Youth Organization of Brooklyn, representing some 125,000 kids, withdrew its affiliation with the Dodgers Knothole Club and urged Chandler to do something about Durocher.

And there was more.

While the feud was simmering and the Dodgers set up camp in Panama, some members of the team's Southern contingent, including out-fielder Dixie Walker, pitcher Kirby Higbe, catcher Bobby Bragan and second baseman Eddie Stanky, circulated a petition announcing their opposition to playing with Robinson.

Rickey got wind of it and immediately had Durocher intervene. He roused the whole team at midnight. While most previous accounts of the meeting, which stem from later interviews given by Harold Parrott, state that Durocher claimed, "I manage this team. I say he plays," in recent interviews several players who attended the meeting disagree. According to them, Durocher, while still dressed in his bathrobe, told the Dodgers that, "If the old man [Rickey] wants him to play, he's going to play," adding, "he can make us all rich," and if they didn't like it, Rickey would arrange for them to be traded. A day later, Rickey met with the petitioners and repeated the offer. Within a year, all four were gone from Brooklyn.

Things came to a head just as the Royals arrived in Panama. Durocher had to return to California to appear at a court hearing that was considering the legality of Day's divorce, and subsequently, her marriage to Durocher.

Dodgers players had their first look at Robinson on March 17. In a 1-1 tie with the Royals, Jackie cracked two hits off pitcher Hal Gregg and fielded his position flawlessly. There were few witnesses to his deeds. Before the Royals arrival, the Dodgers shipped many players, including some of the petitioners, back to Havana.

When the two teams met on March 20 for

game two of the series, fewer than twenty Dodgers remained. They saw Robinson beat out two bunts, but his wild throw to the plate in the first led to three Dodger runs in their eventual 10-3 win. So much for Rickey's plans.

Camp then adjourned back to Havana. Durocher returned with Larraine Day in tow, and the Dodgers played several exhibitions against Cuban teams before entertaining the Royals in another exhibition series beginning on March 26.

Rickey again hoped to showcase Robinson, but his own poor planning ruined it. Left to forage on his own for meals, Robinson came down with an attack of dysentery and missed the first game, a 6-0 Dodgers win, as Howie Schultz spanked out three hits. The next day, as Rickey flew to Florida to meet with Chandler over the whole Durocher/MacPhail matter, Leo dropped a bombshell. Speaking to Ross McGowan, Durocher expressed dissatisfaction with the team's power. The solution, he proposed, would be a trade for Johnny Mize of the Giants, a first baseman. Apparently, Durocher was not yet sold on Robinson, and Jackie did nothing to help himself when he made his first appearance in front of Durocher the next day. Although he singled in the first, again off Hal Gregg, his two errors led to four Dodgers runs. The Royals lost, 5-2.

On March 29, Robinson responded with a repeat performance. Still weakened by his stomach condition, he managed a single and a stolen base, but made two more errors as the Royals lost again, 7-0.

The Dodgers were concerned, both about Robinson and about what to do at first base. Wrote the *Herald Tribune's* Bob Cooke, "the more one sees of the Dodgers in spring training the more acute the first base problem becomes. At least that's the impression of one qualified observer who wishes to remain anonymous."

Robinson sat out the next game before returning to the Royals lineup on March 31—as a sec-

ond baseman. Rickey watched from the stands while Durocher inexplicably left before the game got under way. Supposedly, Montreal Manager Clay Hopper wanted to take a look at first baseman Kevin Conners, but Ross McGowan summed up the feeling of many observers when he wrote "[the move] naturally brought wonderment as to whether his trial at first base—for a possible promotion to the Dodgers—has ended."

Things were getting strange. Cooke began his report from camp as if writing from a ship adrift at sea. "Log of the good ship Dodger. Fortieth day. Men grumbling. Complain about manager leaving ball park early during games with Montreal. Hot weather also bothering men . . .

"Hope to make States in another week. Expect to sight land 'Florida' next Monday morning. A Mariner, more or less ancient, name of Branch Rickey, board ship yesterday. Still have enough food to keep squad alive and Rickey talking."

Rickey now seemed to concur with McGowan's earlier appraisal. After the game he claimed to have tried to work a trade with another National League team that was "the largest offer ever made in baseball." But it was turned down. Rickey may have been trying to dump the four conspirators, including Stanky, all at once, perhaps in exchange for the Mize and several others. If so, Robinson would suddenly have been his second baseman. Rickey may have been showcasing Robinson at second for the benefit of the Brooklyn players. Durocher's odd disappearance may have been indicative of his own displeasure at Rickey's manipulations.

Durocher returned the next day but Robinson stayed at second as the Royals lost yet again. Then Robinson returned to first. Now Rickey admitted that Robinson's shift to second had been made so the Dodgers could see what a fine second baseman he was, but the circumstances seem to indicate that Rickey was as yet unsure where Robinson would eventually play.

Over the next several days, the confusion only increased. On April 4, first baseman Robinson hurt his back in a collision with Brooklyn catcher Bruce Edwards and was sidelined again. He watched from the sidelines as the Dodgers and Royals concluded their series in Havana on April 6.

As the Dodgers embarked on a brief barnstorming trip through the South, Robinson and Campanella were sent ahead to Brooklyn, where the Dodgers and Royals were scheduled to play exhibitions on April 9 and 10. Since the Dodgers players had failed to call for Robinson's promotion, Rickey reportedly decided to have Durocher call for Robinson's promotion while the two teams played in Brooklyn. Then Happy Chandler dropped a bombshell. On the morning of April 9 Chandler announced a decision concerning Durocher and the Dodgers battle with MacPhail. He suspended Durocher for the 1947 season.

Given the impending Robinson situation, his decision appeared odd then and appears even more so today. For if Chandler was as supportive of Rickey as he later claimed, to suspend Durocher was, to be kind, curious. Durocher really hadn't done anything worthy of a suspension, and the timing makes it all the more suspect. It is hard to believe that Chandler made such a decision without considering the impact it might have had on Robinson. Rickey wanted the promotion to appear to be Leo's decision. If it failed, he was off the hook.

Chandler, Durocher and Rickey never admitted that Durocher's suspension had anything to do with Robinson. Yet it may have been a veiled attempt to facilitate that very act. As Wendell Smith wrote only a few days earlier, "The current battle between Rickey and MacPhail is not just an ordinary brawl, nor is it simply because MacPhail allegedly sat between two gamblers . . . MacPhail is against the Rickey-Robinson plan [he] makes thousands of dollars off Negro baseball each year [and] can't stomach the thought of the lily-white

Interim Dodgers Manager Clyde Sukeforth greets Boston Braves Manager Billy Southworth on Opening Day 1947 at Ebbets Field. (National Baseball Library, Cooperstown, N.Y.)

color line being broken." The suspension of Durocher may have been an attempt by Chandler to appease MacPhail at this critical time. He would allow Robinson to be called up, but at the same time it would appear as if he were smacking Rickey and the Dodgers down. Rickey would get what he wanted. So would MacPhail. Durocher would pay.

But another, more ominous scenario may have been taking place. Although Durocher claims in his autobiography that he wanted Robinson from the first time he saw him, the events of spring training and after suggest otherwise. In the autobiography, Durocher admits to knowing nothing about the switch of Robinson to first until just before the start of the season, hardly the sign of a man who was calling the shots. The fact that his later relationship with Robinson was, at best, antagonistic, points to the possibility of trouble between the two.

Durocher either may not have wanted Robinson on the team, may not have wanted him as a starter, or may have chosen to back his veterans. As Ed Stevens recalls, Durocher, "would ride young ballplayers into the ground. He had me so nervous I could hardly come to the ballpark. He wouldn't get on people like Stanky, Pee Wee Reese, Augie Galan, Pete Reiser, Dixie Walker or those kind of people."

Stanky was a team leader and one of Durocher's favorite players. Later, Durocher strongly disagreed with the trade of Stanky, which eventually enabled Robinson to play second. He may have first voiced his opposition to that plan while still in Cuba. Or Durocher may have even wanted Robinson, but as a utility player only. The suspension may have been a convenient way for Rickey to remove Durocher from the situation and take control without making it appear that Robinson's promotion was causing any dissension on the club.

We will probably never know what really hap-pened, as Durocher, Chandler and Rickey have all died. But what seems clear today is that it is highly unlikely that Durocher's suspension was entirely unrelated to the Robinson situation.

The suspension knocked speculation over Robinson's fate off the front pages of sports sections around the country. He was back on the next day.

With Clyde Sukeforth at the temporary helm of the Dodgers, and confusion reigning in Dodgerdom, Brooklyn and Montreal met at Ebbets Field. Earlier that day, Rickey had told Robinson this would be his last game with the Montreal Royals. In the sixth inning, with a man on first, Robinson bunted the ball back to the pitcher for a double play. As he turned to run back into the dugout, he was surprised to see his Montreal teammates applauding and waving. Then he realized what had happened.

Rickey had made the decision public, releasing a brief statement to the press that read only, "The Brooklyn Dodgers today purchased the contract of Jackie Roosevelt Robinson from the Montreal Royals. He will report immediately."

It Was a Great Day in Jersey

Taken from The Sports Beat in
The Pittsburgh Courier

by Wendell Smith

Jersey City, N.J.—The sun smiled down brilliantly in picturesque Roosevelt Stadium here Thursday afternoon and an air of excitement prevailed throughout the spacious park, which was jammed to capacity with 25,000 jabbering, chattering opening day fans . . . A seething mass of humanity, representing all segments of the crazy-quilt we call America, poured into the magnificent ball park they named after a man from Hyde Park—Franklin D. Roosevelt—to see Montreal play Jersey City and the first two Negroes in modern baseball history perform, Jackie Robinson and Johnny Wright . . . There was the usual fanfare and color, with Mayor Frank Hague chucking out the first ball, the band music, kids from Jersey City schools putting on an exhibition of running, jumping, and acrobatics . . . There was also the hot dogs,

peanuts and soda pop . . . And some guys in the distant bleachers whistled merrily: "Take Me Out to the Ball Game" . . . Wendell Wilkie's "One World" was right here on the banks of the Passaic River.

The outfield was dressed in gaudy green, and the infield was as smooth and clean as a new-born babe . . . And everyone sensed the significance of the occasion as Robinson and Wright marched with the Montreal team to deep centerfield for the raising of the Stars and Stripes and the "Star-Spangled Banner" . . . Mayor Hague strutted proudly with his henchmen flanking him on the right and left . . . While the two teams, spread across the field, marched side by side with military precision and the band played on . . . We all stood up—25,000 of us—when the band struck up the National Anthem . . . And we sang lustily and freely, for this was a great day . . . Robinson and Wright stood out there with the rest of the players and dignitaries, clutching their blue-crowned base-

ball caps, standing erect and as still as West Point cadets on dress parade.

What Were They Thinking About?

No one will ever know what they were thinking right then, but I have traveled more than 2,000 miles with their courageous pioneers during the past nine weeks—from Sanford, Fla. to Daytona Beach to Jersey City—and I feel that I know them probably better than any newspaperman in the business . . . I know that their hearts throbbed heavily and thumped a steady tempo with the big drum that was pounding out the rhythm as the flag slowly crawled up the centerfield mast.

And then there was a tremendous roar as the flag reached its crest and unfurled gloriously in the brilliant April sunlight . . . The 25,000 fans settled back in their seats, ready for the ball game as the Jersey City Giants jogged out to their positions . . . Robinson was the second batter and as he strolled to the plate the crowd gave him an enthusiastic reception . . . They were for him . . . They all knew how he had overcome many obstacles in the deep South, how he had been barred from playing in Sanford, Fla., Jacksonville, Savannah and Richmond . . . And yet, through it all, he was standing at the plate as the second baseman of the Montreal team . . . The applause they gave so willingly was a salute of appreciation and admiration . . . Robinson then socked a sizzler to the shortstop and was thrown out by an eyelash a first base.

The second time he appeared at the plate marked the beginning of what can develop into a great career. He got his first hit as a member of the Montreal Royals . . . It was a mighty home run over the left field fence . . . With two mates on the base paths, he walloped the first pitch that came his way and there was an explosive "crack" as bat and ball met . . . The ball glistened brilliantly in the afternoon sun as it went hurtling high and far over the leftfield fence . . . And, the white flag on the foulline pole in left fluttered lazily as the ball whistled by.

He Got a Great Ovation From Team, Fans

Robinson jogged around the bases—his heart singing, a broad smile on his beaming bronze face as his two teammates trotted homeward ahead of him . . . When he rounded third, Manager Clay Hopper, who as coaching there, gave him a heavy pat on the back and shouted: "That's the way to hit that ball!" . . . Between third and home-plate he received another ovation from the stands, and then the entire Montreal team stood up and welcomed him to the bench . . . White hands slapping him on his broad back . . . Deep Southern voices from the bench shouted, "Yo sho' hit 'at one, Robbie, nice goin' kid!" . . . Another said: "Them folks 'at wouldn't let you play down in Jacksonville should be hee'ah now. Whoopee!" . . . And still another: "They cain't stop ya now, Jackie, you're really goin' places and we're going to be right there with ya!" . . . Jackie Robinson laughed softly and smiled . . . Johnny Wright, wearing a big blue pitcher's jacket, laughed and smiled . . . And, high up in the press box, Joe Bostic of the Amsterdam News and I looked at each other knowingly, and, we, too, laughed and smiled . . . Our hearts beat just a bit faster, and the thrill ran through us like champagne bubbles . . . It was a great day in baseball!

But he didn't stop there, this whirlwind from California's gold coast . . . He ran the bases like a wild colt from the Western plains. He laid down two perfect bunts and slashed a hit into rightfield . . . He befuddled the pitchers, made them balk when he was roaring up and down the base paths, and demoralized the entire Jersey City team . . . He was a hitting demon and a base-running maniac . . . The crowd gasped in amazement . . . The opposing pitchers shook their heads in helpless agony . . . His understanding teammates cheered him on with unrivaled enthusiasm . . . And Branch Rickey, the man who had the fortitude and courage to sign him, heard the phenomenal news via telephone in the offices of the Brooklyn Dodgers at Ebbets Field and said admiringly—"He's a wonderful boy, that Jackie Robinson—a wonderful boy!"

They Mobbed Him After the Game

When the game ended and Montreal had chalked up a 14 to 1 triumph, Robinson dashed for the club-house and the showers . . . But before he could get there he was surrounded by a howling mob of kids, who came streaming out of the bleachers and stands . . . They swept down upon him like a great ocean wave and he was downed in a sea of adolescent enthusiasm . . . There he was—this Pied Piper of the diamond—perspiration rolling of his bronze brow, idolizing kids swirling all around him, autograph hounds tugging at him . . . And big cops riding prancing steeds trying unsuccessfully to disperse the mob that had cornered the hero of the day . . . One of his own teammates fought his way through the howling mob and finally "saved" Robinson . . . it was Red Durrett, who was a hero in his own right because he had pounded out two prodigious home runs himself, who came to the "rescue." He grabbed Robinson by the arm and pulled him through the crowd. "Come on," Durrett demanded, "you'll be here all night if you don't fight them off. They'll mob you. You can't possibly sign autographs for all those kids."

So, Jackie Robinson, escorted by the red-head outfielder, finally made his way to the dressing room. Bedlam broke loose in there, too . . . Photographers, reporters, kibitzers and hangers-on fenced him in . . . It was a virtual madhouse . . . His teammates, George Shuba, Stan Breard, Herman Franks, Tom Tatum, Marvin Rackley and all the others, were showering congratulations on him . . . They followed him into the showers, back to his locker and all over the dressing room . . . Flash bulbs flashed and reporters fired questions with machine-gun

like rapidity . . . And Jackie Robinson smiled through it all.

As he left the park and walked out onto the street, the once-brilliant sun was fading slowly in the distant western skies . . . His petite and dainty little wife greeted him warmly and kindly. "You've had quite a day, little man," she said sweetly.

"Yes," he said softly and pleasantly, "God has been good to us today!"

In 1993 Wendell Smith was honored posthumously with the J.G. Taylor Spink Award presented annually by the National Baseball Hall of Fame for "meritorious contributions to baseball writing." It is fitting that the writer who had written the first biography of Jackie Robinson and had served as his most tireless advocate in the African-American press should join Robinson at Cooperstown. Smith was the first African-American member of the Baseball Writers Association of America and wrote for *The Pittsburgh Courier, Chicago American*, and *Chicago Sun-Times*.

ROOKIE OF THE YEAR: 1947

At long last, Jackie Robinson was a Major League Baseball player. Yet he faced challenges beyond those confronted by any of the thousands of men who preceded him into the big leagues. Success on the field would be the least of his worries.

On the morning of April 11, Robinson arrived at Ebbets Field, entered the Brooklyn locker room, was issued uniform number 42 and assigned a locker between Ralph Branca and Gene Hermanski. Reports in mainstream newspapers that morning were surprisingly restrained. Robinson's promotion had long been anticipated, making the actual event somewhat anticlimactic.

Robinson had precious little time to give them any notice. He had to play ball. He and Rachel moved into the McAlpin Hotel and Jackie made his first appearance in a Dodger uniform in the annual three-game exhibition series against the New York Yankees.

Interim Manager Clyde Sukeforth wasted no time installing Robinson in the lineup. Ed Stevens and Howie Schultz had shared first base the day before. Now they sat on the bench as Robinson took over, batting sixth.

Jackie went hitless in his debut. But he did reach base twice on errors, hit one ball on the nose to outfielder Johnny Lindell, pulled a foul into the left field stands, managed a sacrifice and knocked in three runs. The Dodgers won, 14-6.

Even on this day, Robinson's on-field performance was only part of the story. As would be the case for the remainder of his inaugural season, what took place outside the box score was often just as important as what took place in the game

Jackie Robinson as a twenty-eight-year-old rookie in 1947. He would soon become an American legend, lead the Dodgers to the World Series and win Rookie of the Year honors. (Transcendental Graphics)

itself. On this first day, Brooklyn fans gave him a warm welcome. His teammates were polite, but understandably aloof. The nearest thing to a racial incident was the obvious snub by Lee MacPhail, who chose not to attend the game.

Post-game reviews were positive. Most reporters echoed Stanley Woodward in the *Herald Tribune*, who wrote simply "Mr. Robinson has it."

In the second game of the series, Robinson drove in the lone Brooklyn run with a fourth-inning single off Allie Reynolds in the Dodgers 6-1 loss. The next day, he was moved to second in the batting order and contributed a first-inning single and knocked in two more runs. The Dodgers lost again, 10-9 before 30,000 fans in Yankee Stadium.

The 1947 Brooklyn Dodgers were not quite the team of "Boys of Summer" fame, with Gil Hodges and Duke Snider still toiling in the minor leagues. Coming out of the war, no team in baseball was quite sure of itself, as returning veterans tried to bump much younger, much older, or more fortunate incumbents from their jobs. To accommodate the vets, baseball allowed teams to carry forty players for the first several weeks of the season.

Despite finishing only two games out of first place in 1946, the Dodgers began the 1947 season in disarray. Spring training had been a confusing disaster. The teams' self-imposed exile in Cuba left the club virtually untested against big league competition. Durocher's suspension and the anxiety over Robinson made a bad situation even worse.

The Dodgers opened the season with no set lineup, batting order or pitching rotation. Reese and Stanky had short and second pinned down, Bruce Edwards was the regular catcher, and everyone presumed that Dixie Walker and Pete Reiser were set in the outfield, but third base and the other outfield spot were still unsettled.

Robinson was at first, but Stevens and Schultz remained on the roster. If Robinson were to stumble, they could resume their platoon.

The Dodgers opened the regular season on Tuesday, April 15 in Brooklyn against the Boston Braves. Outside Ebbets Field vendors hawked baseball shaped buttons bearing the inscription "I'm for Jackie," while a subdued crowd of 26,623 turned out to watch the first African-American to ever play in an official Major League Baseball game.

The game, itself, was uneventful, at least as far as Robinson's play was concerned. He went hitless and grounded into a double play as Pete Reiser keyed a 5-3 Dodger win.

In Robinson's second game he collected his first hit on a well placed bunt down the third base line, but that was the extent of his contribution as the Dodgers won for the second time, 14-6.

That game marked the end of Clyde Sukeforth's tenure as Dodgers manager. Rickey selected sixty-year-old Burt Shotton to run the Dodgers, giving him the title "managerial consultant" in Durocher's stead. The former outfielder and ex-manager of the Phillies had previously worked for Rickey in the Cardinal organization and was a Dodgers scout. As opposed to the recently departed Durocher, Rickey knew he could count on the mild-mannered Shotton to follow his directives precisely and perform his job quietly. That included playing Jackie Robinson.

Robinson greeted his new manager with a string of good performances. In a 10-4 loss to the Giants on April 18 at the Polo Grounds, Jackie cracked a home run off Dave Koslo, blooped a single, and hit into a line drive double play. The next day Robinson continued to impress. Although the Dodgers lost again, he had three hits, including a line drive single off the leg of New York pitcher Monte Kennedy, and a double off the third base bag.

Jackie continued to play well when the

Robinson is greeted by fans at Ebbets Field prior to the exhibition game against the Yankees which saw him become the first African-American in organized baseball since the 19th century. (UPI, *Courtesy of The Boston Herald*)

Dodgers returned to Brooklyn for a three game set with Philadelphia. The Dodgers won all three, as Robinson scored the Dodgers lone run in a 1-0 win in the first game, collected two hits in the second, and another in the third.

Once again, the box scores don't tell the whole story. For the first time since his arrival in the big leagues, Robinson learned just how difficult his task was going to be. Philadelphia Manager Ben Chapman was from the old school and the Old South. In his fifteen years in the major leagues, Chapman had hit .302, shared the Yankees out-field with Babe Ruth, and even spent two seasons in Brooklyn during the war as a pitcher. He also earned a reputation as an anti-Semite and a racist. In Chapman's world, rookies were put on the face of the earth to be verbally harassed, and blacks didn't belong in the big leagues or anywhere else. He ordered his club to challenge Robinson "to see if he could take it."

For all nine innings of all three games Robinson was on the receiving end of a ceaseless torrent of abuse. And for all three games Robinson took it. It proved too much for some of his teammates to han-dle, and they began to rally around him. In the third game, Eddie Stanky challenged the Phillies to, "Pick on somebody who can answer back." Howie Schultz recalls that, "it was as bad as you can imagine. If they said those things today, it would cause a Civil War."

Rickey met with Chapman and Philadelphia General Manager Herb Pennock after game one of the series, reportedly talking trade. Whether or not Rickey and Chapman also discussed the Phillies bench-jockeying is unclear, but Chapman missed the last game of the series for an undis-closed reason. Nevertheless, the Phillies didn't let up on Robinson. It wasn't until reports of the Phillies behavior appeared in the press did base-ball react. National League President Ford Frick called Chapman on the carpet and ordered the verbal vendetta to cease.

The barrage of insults bothered Robinson, as did his inability to do anything about it. Turning the other cheek was not his natural response, and doing so was difficult. While he eventually learned to channel his anger into his play on the field, he had not yet mastered that ability.

When the Giants followed the Phillies into Brooklyn, Robinson slumped. He failed to col-lect a hit in three games and came up with a sore arm. His poor performance even emboldened some racist Brooklyn fans, whose comments caused the Dodgers to remove microphones designed to pick up crowd noise for their radio broadcasts.

After the Philadelphia series, word quickly made its way around the league that Robinson could be bothered. He was tested at every oppor-tunity.

As the pressure on Jackie mounted, so did the level of harassment. Chicago followed the Giants into Brooklyn on April 29. The Cubs allegedly voted to go on strike before the game, only to be informed by a telegraph from Frick that any strik-ers would be barred for life. They found another way.

In Robinson's first at bat, Cub pitcher Paul Erickson knocked him down several times then finally made contact. Although he failed to give up a run, the Cubs quickly removed Erickson from the lineup before Robinson or anyone else could retaliate. Jackie went hitless in three subse-quent at bats, stretching his hitless streak to twen-ty at bats, although he was twice robbed of hits on infield line drives.

Robinson's batting average was a paltry .227. Since he wasn't getting on base, the other part of his game, his speed, was going to waste. At first base, he was still learning the position and was barely adequate. Although no one was saying so publicly, Robinson was close to being benched. Schultz and Stevens remained in reserve. Only the fact that the Dodgers had jumped out to a 9-3

Robinson is shown in his first major league appearance, an exhibition game against the Yankees.
(UPI, Courtesy of The Boston Herald)

start—due primarily to their surprising pitching—kept his slump from becoming a major issue.

To his credit, Robinson refused to get drawn into a battle with the opposition, writing in his "Jackie Says" column in the *Courier* that the bench-jockeying and knockdown "really didn't bother me." Robinson was wise enough to know that admission otherwise would only fuel more such activity and ensure that any subsequent black players would face the same problem.

In the final two games of the Cubs series he finally broke free and collected three hits. But when the Cardinals came into Brooklyn on May 6, there was more trouble.

In a copywritten column that appeared two days later, Stanley Woodward of the *New York Herald Tribune* broke a story that claimed the Cardinals had planned to go on strike, due to Robinson, before the first game of the series. According to Woodward, only the intervention of National League President Ford Frick and Cardinal President Sam Breadon averted the walkout. Woodward wrote that Frick told the players bluntly "If you do this, you will be suspended from the league . . . I don't care if half the league strikes. . . all will be suspended and I don't care if it wrecks the National League for five years."

Subsequent research by a number of writers and historians have since cast doubt on whether or not the Cardinals did, in fact, vote to strike that day. Surviving players have denied the story, although their reticence in regard to the incident is understandable: few players of the era admit to the prejudice of their earlier years.

It is tenable that Woodward, perhaps in collusion with Frick and Rickey, created the tale and floated the story to send a message to other clubs throughout the league. Whether true or not, it received national coverage and effectively sent a warning to every player in the major leagues that organized action against Robinson would bring dire consequences.

Then everything took a more ominous tone.

The press reported that Robinson was the subject of numerous death threats. So when the Dodgers went into Philadelphia on May 9, the Phillies, muzzled by Frick, reacted by holding their baseball bats like rifles, aiming at Robinson and imitating gunfire.

On the field, Robinson's position was made more secure that day when the Dodgers sold Howie Schultz to Philadelphia, although Ed Stevens remained on the roster. Robinson responded by breaking completely out of his slump, as he battered Phillie pitching for eight hits as the Dodgers dropped three of four to the team from the "City of Brotherly Love."

The Dodgers next traveled to Cincinnati, where Robinson received so many death threats that the FBI searched nearby rooftops for snipers. Burt Shotton warned the team of the danger they faced during a clubhouse meeting. According to outfielder Gene Hermanski, when Shotton finished and asked if anyone on the team had any suggestions, Hermanski quipped, "Yeah, I've got one. Why don't we all wear the same number— Forty-two? That kind of broke up the tension."

During all this time, Branch Rickey stayed in the background, offering Robinson his private support, but leaving him to fight his own battles. Yet he was still indulging in more of his "plans."

First baseman Ed Stevens had made only a few pinch-hitting appearances. As Stevens remembers, he was in Cincinnati when, "Mr. Rickey talked to me and told me, 'The job is yours. You've made the club. But will you do a favor for the ball club? Let me play Jackie Robinson at first, you stay in shape at Montreal, and I will promise you with a handshake that [in 1948] I'll get rid of Eddie Stanky, put Jackie back on second, and you've got a job for the next ten or fifteen years, as long as your ability holds.'

"I told him 'Well Mr. Rickey, I've already got the ball club made, I don't see why I have to leave this club.' He said, 'I'm asking as a favor to me. And I'll take care of you if you do this for me.'

"Well [I was] twenty-two years old, no agents, nobody to talk to, so I agreed with him to go to Montreal."

Like Schultz, Stevens is to be admired. For both incumbent first basemen "turned the other cheek," and stood aside, allowing Rickey to bring Robinson into the big leagues unfettered by any more controversy. It was particularly difficult for Stevens, who was a native of Galveston, Texas. He recalls that, "I really took a beating by the old timers down there. And, there's no bitterness in me. But the old timers in my hometown of Galveston, just ridiculed the life out of me for letting a black man take my job. I was just over twenty years-old trying to fight all that stuff off . . .". Rickey got what he wanted, then conve-

Robinson is shown in his first major league appearance, an exhibition game against the Yankees. He takes a pick-off throw as Johnny Lindell slides back to first base.
(UPI, *Courtesy of The Boston Herald*)

National League President Ford Frick, shown here with his wife, informed the St. Louis Cardinals that he would suspend for five years any player who refused to play against Robinson. (Courtesy of The Boston Herald)

niently forgot all about his promise the following winter, and eventually sold Stevens to the Pittsburgh Pirates.

In the face of continuing resistance from the other NL clubs, Stevens' demotion sent a clear message—Jackie Robinson was going to play first base for Brooklyn, no matter what. On May 14, as Stevens traveled north, Robinson extended his post-slump hitting streak to eleven games and raised his average to .290 with an infield single in the series finale to Cincinnati, a 2-0 Dodgers loss.

Yet while Robinson regained his hitting stroke, the Dodgers stumbled. Although they trailed the first place Cubs by only two games, the proud Dodgers were in fifth place.

In one regard, Rickey's decision to bring Robinson to the major leagues was a resounding success; one that had every team in the National League smiling. When Jackie Robinson came to town, the ballparks filled up. Coverage of Robinson in the black press helped immeasurably.

Many, like the *Courier*, ran special sidebars each week listing Robinson's statistics while providing in-depth coverage of recent performances.

The result was a huge increase in the number of black faces in the stands around the National League. That made some club owners nervous, but they soon discovered that black fans paid the same money for tickets and bought the same hot dogs and soda. In Chicago on May 18, the second largest crowd in Wrigley Field history at the time—46,572—turned out for the game. A Wednesday afternoon game in St. Louis a week later drew 16,249, double the usual amount. An estimated six thousand black fans were the difference.

Brooklyn continued to struggle for the next month, playing .500 baseball, as the Giants and Braves shared first place. Then the team started to come together.

A number of factors came into play. Robinson and the Dodgers had completed their first road trip, survived it, and now knew what to expect. Shotton was also becoming more familiar with the team, and the questions that remained from spring training were finally being answered. Spider Jorgenson, Robinson's Montreal teammate, wrested third base from Arky Vaughn; Carl Furillo took over the final outfield spot; Pee Wee Reese recovered from an early season slump; and twenty-one-year-old Ralph Branca emerged as the ace of the pitching staff.

The real catalyst for the turnaround was Jackie Robinson. For the first month of the season, he struggled. For the next month, he merely survived. Now, he began to thrive, and the other Dodgers began looking to him as an integral part of the club, a teammate first and a black man second. Not that he was always warmly embraced; there were some Dodgers that year who never truly accepted him. But he had earned their respect. For nine innings every day they put all other feelings aside and fought for a common goal, the National League pennant.

It didn't hurt that he, Rachel and Jackie Jr., moved from the hotel to an apartment in Brooklyn. For the first time, the Robinson's enjoyed some semblance of family life.

On June 14 in a double-header loss to St. Louis, Robinson quietly began a hitting streak, collecting a double in game one and a single in game two. While the Dodgers were crushed again the following day, 11-3, falling to 27-25, Robinson banged out two more hits.

As Brooklyn won five out of their next six, Robinson was in the middle of things, collecting a key base hit, contributing a sacrifice or beating out a bunt to keep a rally alive. He was making a difference. Even in the one game they lost, Robinson still starred. Cincinatti's Ewell Blackwell, fresh off a no-hitter, held the Dodgers hitless into the ninth. With one out, Eddie

When Branch Rickey asked Robinson to "turn the other cheek," it meant having to endure photo opportunities such as the one with Phillies Manager Ben Chapman. Chapman was one of Robinson's chief tormentors in his rookie season.
(Courtesy of The Boston Herald)

Despite a great season in 1947, Robinson was left off the All-Star team in favor of Stan Musial, who was hitting just .241 at the **break.** *(Transcendental Graphics)*

Stanky singled to break up the no-hitter. Robinson was up next. An infuriated Blackwell aimed his ire at Robinson and sent the next pitch at his head. Robinson got up, dusted himself off, and smacked the next strike into center field for a "take that" base hit.

In Pittsburgh on June 24, the Dodgers finally saw the player who had terrorized the International League a year before. Pirate hurler Fritz Ostermueller and Ralph Branca were dueling to a 2-2 tie in the fifth when Robinson singled, stole a base and moved to third. On Ostermueller's first pitch, Robinson faked a dash home. The pitcher glanced disdainfully over at Robinson, yelled something, then toed the rubber in position to take a full wind up. That was all Robinson needed.

Jackie timed the pitcher's slow-motion windup perfectly and raced home, sliding under the tag of his chagrined former Montreal teammate, Dixie Howell. The run proved the difference in the game, and gave Branca his ninth win.

It would not be the first time Robinson did something spectacular in a game pitched by Branca. The rookie pitcher, whose locker was next to Robinson's in the clubhouse, was one of the first players to become close to Robinson. Robinson's more famous friendship with Pee Wee Reese took longer to develop. Some Dodgers always felt that Robinson tried just a little harder in games pitched by Branca.

The Dodgers kept winning and snuck into first two days later. For the next ten days Brooklyn and Boston took turns leading the National League. Robinson's hit streak ended against the Giants in the second game of a July 4 doubleheader. But now the Dodgers led the league with a 41-30 record, 14-6 during Robinson's streak.

One day before, on July 3, Bill Veeck of the Cleveland Indians announced that he had signed infielder Larry Doby of the Newark Eagles. Doby became the second African-American in the major leagues. Robinson was no longer alone. Doby's signing had little direct impact on Jackie, but did send him a message that his struggles were not in vain. He had nudged the door open and now Doby had pressed in behind. Soon, he hoped, a steady stream of black players would follow him. Indeed, within two weeks the St. Louis Browns signed both Hank Thompson and Willard Brown of the Kansas City Monarchs.

The Braves came to Brooklyn on July 5 determined to regain their lead. They won the first contest to draw to a tie, but the Dodgers won the following day to enter the All-Star break with a one-game lead.

Jackie Robinson should have made the National League all-star team in 1947. Johnny Mize of the Giants, whose 24 home runs and 63 RBIs led the major leagues, was the legitimate and correct choice of the fans in this first year of public balloting. But Cardinal Manager Eddie Dyer selected his own first baseman, Stan Musial, as Mize's backup.

In almost any other year, one could not have argued with Dyer's decision. But not in 1947. Musial battled appendicitis early in the season and was hitting only .241 at the break. By contrast, Robinson was hitting .310 and leading the league in runs scored. No other first baseman in the league was even close. Of the other Dodgers selected, Bruce Edwards, Dixie Walker, Eddie Stanky and Pee Wee Reese, none was hitting above .284. Branca made the team as a pitcher.

When the regular season resumed, Robinson picked up where he left off, cracking his fifth home run of the year to provide the margin of victory in a 5-3 win over Chicago. As the Dodgers extended their lead over the rest of the National League, Jackie continued his stellar play. He was taking so many liberties on the bases, it was news when he did not. As Bob Cooke noted in his report of the Dodgers 5-2 win over the

The Cleveland Indians became the first American League team to integrate when Owner Bill Veeck signed Larry Doby from the Newark Eagles on July 3, 1947.
(Courtesy of The Boston Herald)

Reds on July 23: "It was surprising to see him stop at second after Reese's single in the first. As a rule, Robinson stops at second about as infrequently as the Pennsylvania Railroad's Congressional Limited Stops at Rahway, New Jersey." As if to make up for his gaff, two days later in Pittsburgh Jackie scored from second on an infield grounder.

From July 19 to the end of the month Brooklyn won thirteen straight games to take command in the pennant race. They stumbled a bit in early August as St. Louis streaked to within three games, then slowly pulled away again. The

Cardinals were unable to draw closer than 4 $\frac{1}{2}$ games for the remainder of the season, and a six-game St. Louis losing streak in mid-September all but decided the pennant race.

The Dodgers charge over the Cardinals was punctuated by a series of incidents between the two teams involving Robinson. On August 16, Robinson was spiked on the foot by Cardinal outfielder Joe Medwick. Two days later, outfielder Enos Slaughter cut Robinson on the lower leg. While each player denied the bloodshed was deliberate, the Dodgers were infuriated, making their eventual victory over the Cardinals that much sweeter.

Brooklyn signed another black player, pitcher Dan Bankhead, and brought him to Brooklyn on August 26. The signing had nothing to do with providing Robinson a companion. The Dodgers simply wanted to win, and hoped the pitcher would provide some pennant insurance.

Robinson was Mr. Consistency for the remainder of the year, as his average hovered around .300. He had adapted to big league pitching, was learning to hit the curve, and starting to belt the ball with some authority. Jackie finally missed his first game of the season on September 7, the result of an old back injury aggravated by a day at the golf course. He missed two games, as Cookie Lavagetto replaced him at first.

On September 12, *The Sporting News* named Robinson Major League Baseball's "Rookie of the Year," the first player so honored by the award which now bears his name. The paper noted that the choice of Robinson "was on the basis of stark baseball values," lest anyone think the St. Louis-based "Bible of Baseball" had suddenly gone soft. "Robinson was rated and examined solely as a freshman player in the big leagues," the announcement continued, "on the basis of his hitting, his running, his defensive play and his team value."

The selection of Robinson by the conservative-minded tabloid demonstrated just how much Robinson had accomplished. While he was not yet "just another player," he had proved it was possible for a black player to transcend the stereotypes and be appreciated purely for his athletic ability. While Robinson still regularly faced the ire of both fans and opponents, he was clearly winning the battle.

More evidence was provided on September 19. The Dodgers returned from a road trip to find 2,000 fans waiting for them at Pennsylvania Station. While Shorty Lowice's five-piece "Symphony" played a dirge for the Cardinals in the form of "the St. Louis Blues," the Dodgers players left the train only to be enveloped by their zealous fans. No one was more popular than Jackie Robinson, who had to be rescued by a dozen policemen before racing to the Eighth Avenue subway with a pack of admirers in pursuit, a scene reminiscent of what took place in Montreal the previous year.

The Dodgers clinched the pennant on September 22, earning the right to play the Yankees in the World Series. On September 23, Rickey allowed Robinson to be celebrated with a "day" at Ebbets Field, and over 26,000 fans turned out. In a pre-game ceremony, Robinson was given a 1947 Cadillac, a gold watch, a television, silverware and 168 dollars in cash, all of which had come from fan contributions. "Bojangles" Bill Robinson took part in the ceremony. As he handed Robinson the watch, he spoke for millions when he added, "I'm sixty-nine years old and I never thought I'd live to see the day when I'd stand face to face with Ty Cobb in Technicolor."

Brooklyn celebrated the Dodgers again on September 26 with a parade through the streets that drew 500,000. When Robinson was introduced before the crowd at Brooklyn's Borough Hall, he received the largest cheers of the day as he picked up the rookie award from *Sporting News* President J. G. Taylor Spink.

The Dodgers finished the regular season with a record of 94-60, five games ahead of second

On August 26, 1947 the Dodgers signed their second African-American player, pitcher Dan Bankhead, who is shown here signing autographs for young fans at Ebbets Field.
(Courtesy of The Boston Herald)

The 1947 Dodgers starting infield of (l-r) Spider Jorgensen, Pee Wee Reese, Eddie Stanky and Jackie Robinson.
(National Baseball Library, Cooperstown, N.Y.)

place St. Louis. Depth, speed and defense carried the team to the title, as forty-three different position players appeared in the lineup. Ralph Branca won 21 games and Hugh Casey saved 18, and despite a lack of power, every Dodgers regular, except for Eddie Stanky, hit .274 or better, and Stanky supplemented his .254 mark with 103 walks, second best in the league to Pee Wee Reese's 104 as the Dodgers set an NL record with 732 walks.

Robinson slumped the last week, finishing the season with a .297 average, third best on the club behind Pete Reiser's .309 and Dixie Walker's .306. His 125 runs scored tied Ted Williams for the major league lead, and his 29 stolen bases trailed only Bob Dillinger of the St. Louis Browns. Robinson's twelve home runs tied him with Reese

for the team lead and his slugging percentage of .427 was second on the club to Carl Furillo.

He also won over his Dodgers teammates, as Cleveland sportswriter Gordon Cobbledick noted late in the year that Jackie's teammates now viewed him with "something approaching genuine warmth and affection." Even Dixie Walker paid him tribute, telling *The Sporting News* late in the year that, "No other ballplayer on the club, with the possible exception of Bruce Edwards, has done more to put the Dodgers up in the race than Robinson has. He is everything Branch Rickey said he was when he came up from Montreal."

Robinson's value was apparent to anyone who had the opportunity to watch him play that season. He later finished fifth in balloting for the Baseball Writers of America's MVP award, trailing only winner Bob Elliott of the Braves, Johnny Mize, Ewell Blackwell and Edwards.

When the World Series opened on September 30 in New York, the Yankees were heavily favored. A record crowd of more than 73,000 turned out for game one at Yankee Stadium.

In this first Series at-bat, Robinson provided an earmark of his performance in subsequent Series. Time and time again, Robinson got the Dodgers going, collecting the first hit, scoring the first run or becoming the first base runner. So, it was this day in New York.

In the top of the first with one out, Robinson drew a walk off starter Spec Shea then took advantage of rookie catcher Yogi Berra and easily stole second. Then Jackie made a rare mistake. Reiser tapped back to the box, Robinson broke for third and got caught in a run down.

Using his quickness, Robinson avoided being tagged out long enough to allow Reiser to get to second. He scored on Walker's single to put the Dodgers up, 1-0.

In the third, Robinson walked again. He rattled Shea into a balk, sending him to second, where he was left stranded.

Branca had a perfect game through four innings, but came apart in the fifth, giving up five runs and failing to record a single out. That was the game, as the Yankees held on to win, 5-2.

They went up two games to none the next day. New York scored first, then Brooklyn tied the score in the third when Robinson's two-out single—his first World Series hit—scored Pee Wee Reese. The Yankees eventually won, 10-3, although Robinson collected his second hit in the eighth, a double.

Jackie started the Dodgers off in Game Three with a first-inning single. He stole his second base of the Series, and when catcher Sherm Lollar's low throw dribbled past Phil Rizzuto, Jackie started for second, only to be doubled up by Snuffy Stirnweiss, who alertly backed up the play.

Brooklyn broke the game open in the second with six runs, chasing Yankees starter Bobo Newsom. It was a typical Dodgers rally, as the team took advantage of a walk, a series of base hits, including a single by Robinson, and some aggressive baserunning to score six times without a homer. New York clawed back, but the Dodgers held on to win, 9-8.

Game Four was one of the most famous in the history of the World Series, as Yankee hurler Bill Bevens held the Dodgers hitless into the ninth. Bevens was wild, and in the fifth the Dodgers pushed across a run with two walks, a sacrifice and a fielder's choice. But with Pee Wee Reese on third, Robinson struck out.

The Yankees led 2-1 in the ninth. With one out, Bevens walked Carl Furillo and pinch runner Al Gionfriddo stole second. Bevens then walked Reiser, and Cookie Lavagetto, pinch hitting for Eddie Stanky, smacked a double off the right field wall, just out of reach of Tommy Henrich, to put his name into the history books

On September 23, Brooklyn fans honored Robinson with a special day of tributes. Among the gifts he received were a gold watch, silverware, a television, cash and the Cadillac shown in the photo. Jackie is with his wife Rachel and his friend and Hollywood star, Bill "Bojangles" Robinson.
(Transcendental Graphics)

The postseason highlight for the 1947 Dodgers was the dramatic ninth inning double hit by Cookie Lavagetto (center) which broke up Yankees starter Bill Bevens' no-hitter and drove in two runs as the Dodgers won Game Four by a 3-2 score and evened the Series at two games apiece.
(Courtesy of The Boston Herald)

and deliver Brooklyn a win on its only hit of the game.

In Game Five the Yankees won behind Spec Shea's five-hitter, giving them a three games to two lead. DiMaggio's fifth-inning home run was the difference. The Dodgers scored their lone run in the sixth when Robinson singled in Gionfriddo.

Facing elimination, the Dodgers refused to die, winning Game Six 8-6. Robinson helped Brooklyn score four runs with a first-inning single and third-inning double. But the day belonged to Al Gionfriddo. His snag of DiMaggio's sixth-inning drive to left center snuffed out a Yankee rally. Hugh Casey notched a save with a clutch ninth-inning pitching performance.

But the Yankees were still the Yankees. They won Game Seven and the Series as Joe Page shut down Brooklyn 5-2 with five innings of stellar relief work. Robinson went hitless in the loss.

Even in defeat, Robinson still gained some kind of victory. He played well in the Series, leading the Dodgers with seven hits, and demonstrated that he was a key player in the Brooklyn attack. To take the vaunted Yankees to seven games was an accomplishment no team had attained since the 1926 St. Louis Cardinals.

The season was over, and the experiment complete, an achievement that ultimately meant far more than any world championship. The Dodgers may have lost, but Jackie Robinson, and ultimately, America, had won a larger victory.

Jackie Robinson and the Hollywood Integration Film

by Gerald Early

It is a virtual truism that the commercial films largely deal with a prescribed set of cultural and social day dreams. That is to say that certain kinds of real problems and real issues that a society is dealing with at any given moment are fantasized about, worked through (with plausible or implausible premises) and resolved (plausibly or implausibly) in commercial films. Films of a given era or epoch, no matter how ineptly made or how far-fetched or how seemingly removed from reality, are about what is on a society's mind at the time, a dramatization of that society's fears and hopes, its obsessions and conventions. The characters in any given film become archetypes that have a particular resonance with that society, not because of the way the character develops but because of values the character represents. The plots are not realistic re-enactments of a situation or a set of situations but rather a mythological representation of some set dilemma of the hero or the victim.

It is a fact of American history that from 1945, the end of the Second World War, onward race relations dominated the domestic scene in a way comparable to the turbulent period known as the Reconstruction. There are several reasons for this: first, the Second World War was fought against a political ideology—Nazism—that was built on the ideas of white supremacy and genocide. Racist concepts about inferior and superior races, racial destinies, and the like became abhorrent as they were associated with something inescapably pathological. This, coupled with the writings and teachings of sociologists and anthropologists that stressed both that race as an idea had no scientific validity and that the standard of cultural relativism was the only fair way to understand how other people lived, led to the beginnings of a wide-spread discrediting of racism as a popularly accepted intellectual notion about the meaning of human difference. The United States, a country built on the idea of white supremacy, but also a democracy that espoused the belief that all people were created equal, has always found itself in an embarrassing ideological contradiction that the war against Nazism and fascism simply exacerbated. Second, blacks had become, by 1945, an important, urban population in the United States, more effective as a political pressure group, and with a growing economic importance as consumer group. The tremendous prosperity the United States enjoyed during the Cold War years of the 1940s, 1950s, and 1960s further insured both the growing consumer power of blacks and the growing intensity of their pressure tactics to bring about a change in their status as one of America's most stigmatized and degraded ethnic groups.

That someone like Jackie Robinson would emerge as a national figure in 1945 and become by 1947 one of the most famous men in America, and, more important, a hero of near mythical proportions, when one considers how much of a presence race relations assumed as an issue in America, is not surprising. There are several remarkable facets of the appearance of Robinson but the three most important are these: First, he joined together political and social issues to the world of popular culture because his significance in the world of popular culture, like the seminal black athletes before him, Jesse Owens, Jack Johnson, and Joe Louis, was largely political. (Robinson was a very good ballplayer but he is not remembered merely for that reason). Second, he was the first angry black man to become a popular culture and heroic icon. (Not even Jack Johnson, the first black heavyweight champion, and a figure of some social notoriety in his day, could be accurately described as an angry black man although, to be sure, he was a rebellious one. It must be remembered that Robinson became a public figure at the time when a music called Be-Bop was being created by young rebellious jazz musicians like Charlie Parker, Dizzy Gillespie, Thelonious Monk, John Lewis, and others. It was a music that signified new militancy in African-American culture as a whole. Robinson did not create this mood, rather he was a reflection of it. By the middle 1950s, one of the most famous jazz musicians in America was trumpeter Miles Davis, very dark-skinned, like Robinson, with a persona of the angry black man that made virtually a romanticized figure). Finally, Robinson became the first national heroic figure associated with the drama of racial integration. For a long time, he, as an image and symbol, gave the struggle for integration its character of self-sacrifice and nobility. This is largely because of the agreement he reached with Branch Rickey not to retaliate when he was baited or abused on the field during the real years of his career with the Dodgers. But from the evidence of Rickey's own words in The American Diamond, Robinson displayed anger, even if, for the most part, he never retaliated (although apparently there were a few times when he could not forbear):

For three years (that was the agreement) this boy was to turn the other cheek. He did, day after day, until he had no other to turn. They were both beat off. There were

slight slip-ups on occasion in that first year in Montreal . . . Righteous impulse caught him unaware a couple times...

It was this unique combination of control and angry resentment that made Robinson seem dignified and manly, heroic to both blacks and whites, in much the way that Joe Louis had been, although Robinson generally gave the public less an impression of sheer stoicism.

Robinson, arguably, had a greater impact on American race relations than any other black athlete before him because he integrated a sport of such tremendous cultural and mythological significance in American life. Even after the Second World War, baseball was the most popular of all spectator sports in America. Because of the existence of a fairly organized set of Negro baseball leagues for over two generations, professional baseball was also the most popular spectator sport among blacks as well. Robinson, in other words, joined together a number of important strands in American culture and came along at an absolutely crucial time when the republic was re-defining its nationalism, its very national identity, against the threat of Soviet Communism. It is no wonder that Robinson who, within three years of his ascent to major league baseball, won both the Rookie of the Year and Most Valuable Player Awards, should be the subject of a Hollywood film. He had become something more than a baseball player. He was part of the cultural daydreams of American life, as Americans, both black and white, contemplated the possibilities of a society where blacks and whites would meet and interact completely as social equals. That he wound starring in his own bio-pic is not so terribly unusual, although, of course,

few athletes have played themselves in films that were primarily about them. (Bill Mathias and Muhummad Ali are two other athletes who immediately come to mind as having played themselves in Hollywood bio pics). In 1950, when The Jackie Robinson Story was released, at the height of Robinson's popularity when he was doubtless the most famous black man in America, who else could have played him? Besides, black athletes like Paul Robeson (who became a notable actor), Joe Louis, Henry Armstrong, and Jack Johnson had appeared in films, so there was nothing new in having Robinson act. Furthermore, many great athletes have launched modest acting or stage careers to cash in on their fame: Babe Ruth, Johnny Weissmuller, Buster Crabbe, Jack Dempsey, Jim Corbett, Babe Didrlkson, to name just a few before Robinson. In the grand machinery of popular culture, performers are almost seen as interchangeable or at least the merchants of popular culture have always thought that fame in one field of entertainment could be credibly transferred to another.

It has typically been the case to see The Jackie Robinson Story in the tradition of the Hollywood baseball bio pic, comparing it to The Pride of the Yankees, The Pride of St. Louis, The Monty Stratton Story, or more troubling baseball biographies, though no less happy in the end, like The Winning Team or Fear Strikes Out. These comparisons are useful. Just as comparisons with the standard Hollywood bio pic of the 1940s and 1950s of any popular culture figure, from Rodgers and Hart (Words and Music), and Benny Goodman (The Benny Goodman Story), to W.C. Handy (St. Louis Blues) and Lillian Roth (I'll Cry Tomorrow). But I believe that The

Jackie Robinson Story can be most fruitfully understood within the tradition of the black Hollywood film. Robinson's presence had an enormous impact on Hollywood, so much so that he became, in essence, a cultural paradigm. He changed the way blacks were conceived in dramatic film.

Before the emergence of Robinson during the Cold War, blacks had three very limited uses in Hollywood film. In an otherwise "white" film, a black actor or a group of them would largely serve as comic relief, stereotypical Sambo-type or Mammies, buffoons or caretakers, roles made famous by Stephin Fetchit, on the one hand, and Hattie McDaniel, on the other. In the standard "black" or all-Negro cast film, such as Green Pastures or Hallelujah or Cabin in the Sky or Stormy Weather, the overall texture conveys the Negro's folksiness or musicality, reworking Victorian minstrelsy. In a drama, like Imitation of Life, Pinky, or Lost Boundaries, we get the stereotypical story of the tragic mulatto, trying to pass for white, a hoary theme as old as antebellum literature. In the early 1940s, Walter White, executive director of the NAACP, had serious discussions with heads of some Hollywood studios about changing the way blacks were depicted on screen, discussions which black actors like McDaniel, Clarence Muse, Stepin Fetchit, who worked with the old stereotypes deplored, fearing it would simply put them out of work. One result of White's push for a new depiction of the Negro was In This Our Life. a 1942 film with Bette Davis and Olivia De Havilland. In it, a black character, wrongly accused and eventually acquitted of killing a child in a hit-and-run accident aspires to be a lawyer. This was the first time in any Hollywood film that a black character expressed such an ambition.

Jackie Robinson intensified this change in Hollywood's depiction of blacks. Robinson gave us the aspiring African-American trying to make it on merit in a sometimes hostile, sometimes concerned white society that doubts his ability. This is explicitly a new black type, prefigured by Joe Louis but fulfilled by Robinson because what he did involved so dramatically interaction with whites. The Jackie Robinson Story opens with a voice-over: "This is the story of a boy and his dream, but more than that it is the story of an American boy and a dream that is truly American." To make a black character represent American values so clearly was also something new in American film. This happened in good measure because Robinson was a baseball player, so tied to a sport which was tied inextricably to American nationalism. In the opening scene, a young Jackie Robinson joins a group of white boys on a field while a couple older whites, young men, hit fungos to them. At first, the white men resent Robinson's asking them to hit fungos to him and try to hit ones that he cannot catch. But Robinson proves himself superior to the other boys, despite the fact he has no glove. The white men are both impressed by his talent, his merit, so they give him a beat-up glove. This opening scene not only sums up the theme of this movie but of all integration dramas of its type: acceptance and proving oneself worthy of it. Politically, in our age of militant multiculturalism and insistence on accepting and respecting the differences of others, this may seem rather timid, almost Kipling-esque. Nonetheless, it was a step forward, portraying black people on the screen not simply in more positive ways but, even more importantly, more complex ways than they had been. Robinson forced the white world to deal with a complex black man and the meaning of his aspiration and ambition. The impact of this cannot be taken lightly. The Jackie Robinson Story is certainly not a good film. It is a white-washed version of Robinson's life as most Hollywood bio pics are white-washed versions of their subjects. Robinson's court-martial is never mentioned; his sense of alienation from the other players in the Negro Leagues is never dealt with (the film has him playing for the Black Panthers, not the Monarchs with whom he actually did play); the difficult nature of his relationship with his brother Mack is never explored; the fact that baseball was not his best sport in college; his testimony before HUAC ends the film but there is no mention of Paul Robeson, whose statement about blacks not be willing to fight in a war against the Soviet Union, was the occasion for Robinson's moment. And of course the film offers no examination of the black community's reaction to Robinson's testimony which was decidedly mixed as Robeson was held in high regard in many black circles. These changes were to be expected in order to make Robinson's life fit the Horatio Alger—Booker T. Washington uplift story of how many white boys saw this movie and, as a result, raised Robinson to their pantheon of baseball heroes. For that is what the film was, radically, about: presenting a black man as a true American hero . The important point here is not that this is not really true for blacks in the 1940s and 1950s but how much Hollywood thought that there was an audience—made up of both blacks and whites—that wanted very much to have that story, needed that story. Robinson's story was about the triumph of western liberalism, where it is possible for society to overcome its own mistakes, to offer opportunity for all its citizens, to progress to ever greater enlightenment.

Robinson as a national figure was the obvious inspiration for films like Home of the Brave, made in 1949, produced by Stanley Kramer and directed by Mark Robeson. This is the story of a black soldier who suffers a nervous breakdown when his white friend is killed while they are both on a reconnaissance mission in the Pacific. Here is a character much like Robinson, highly skilled but among white colleagues who doubt his ability, having to work with a team, forced to fit in, subject to abuse, unable to know truly which whites are his friends and which are not. Robinson was also the clear inspiration for No Way Out the 1950 film starring Sidney Poitier (in his film debut) as a doctor accused by malpractice by the rabidly racist brother of one of his patients. Here we have the Robinson situation being examined mythically in film: a black person in a largely white profession, working in a white hospital, under pressure not only from the nature of the profession itself but from a feeling that his white colleagues may doubt his ability, taunt-

ed by a racist (Poitier's character is called every vile racist name Joseph Mankiewicz, the film's writer and director, could think of), forced to prove his worth. Poitier is saved from criminal charges through an autopsy which proves his diagnosis was correct. (Ironically, he is saved by the dismemberment of a white man's body. This is liberal, northern, scientific justice. We know that the ritual of emotional, fanatical southern justice by lynching is the dismemberment of the black man's body. Mankiewicz was an intellectual enough filmmaker that he may have had this symbolism in mind in making the film). As a doctor, of course, Poitier had to wear a white uniform, just as Robinson must as a ball-player. Also, Poitier was a breakthrough in the image of black males in Hollywood. Not only was he a dramatic actor who played complex black males but he was also extremely dark-skinned, like Robinson. Poitier was to go to other roles in "integration" dramas like Edge of the City, The Defiant Ones, Blackboard Jungle, Lilies of the Field, and The Slender Thread, were he played a black person operating in a largely white world. This type of career, I posit, clearly would not have been possible without the Robinson paradigm.

I do not mean to suggest by any of this that Robinson solved the

problem of the depiction of blacks in Hollywood films by finally providing a heroic paradigm. There is much that is problematic about the Hollywood "integration" film of the Cold War and the black characterizations, though an improvement over the past, are often unsatisfying. For many in the black community these days, Robinson himself as the heroic emblem of integration is a problematic figure, mostly because blacks themselves feel so ambivalent about integration itself as a social and political goal. Too often, the Robinson "integration" hero resembles Uncle Tom, the hero of the famous anti-slavery novel of mid-19th century, who seems to care too much about humanizing or changing whites. Yet there is much about Robinson and the paradigm he created that was and is truly revolutionary, that created space for a dignified black presence in the United States, and advanced the ideal of a society where blacks and whites could work together and that sparked many of the changes for the better that we see in our cultural life today. For those who may complain about the admitted short-comings of Robinson paradigm, they should not lose sight of its grander cultural beauty and epic political significance. But as Holden Caulfield said, "People always clap for the wrong things."

Gerald Early is the Director of African and Afro-American studies and Professor of English at Washington University in St. Louis. He is the author of *Daughters: On Family and Fatherhood* and *The Culture of Bruising*. He was one of the principal contributors to Ken Burns Baseball documentary.

ROBINSON UNBOUND: 1948-1949

With his rookie year completed, over the next two seasons Jackie Robinson would become one of the best, if not the best, players in the game. Yet his struggle was not over, either on or off the field. His experiences in 1948 and 1949 echo the sentiment of the closing words of his autobiography when he wrote, "I was a black man in a white world. I never had it made."

At the completion of the World Series, Robinson began to cash in on the notoriety he had achieved in 1947. He had earned the major league minimum $5,000 in 1947, but suddenly he was one of the games' most marketable players. Only Bob Feller and Stan Musial eventually earned more.

In the middle of the 1947 season, Rickey began to allow Robinson to accept a few commercial offers. Over the final months of the season, he appeared in print ads endorsing a variety of products in the black press, including bread, hats, and although he didn't smoke, cigarettes. At the end of the season he accepted a guarantee of $2,500 per appearance to make a theatrical tour with several vaudeville acts, signed contracts for the first of an eventual four autobiographies, this one ghost-written by Wendell Smith, and agreed to a movie based on his life. He also traveled the country appearing at testimonials and banquets.

Significantly, for the first time since he began playing professional baseball, Jackie did not join a barnstorming team. He was not asked to by the white stars who did so, like Bob Feller, and it no longer served his purpose to play with all black clubs. Besides, after the rigors of his rookie season, he had earned a well-deserved vacation.

Robinson's rookie season success was underscored at the box office. While Brooklyn drew 1,807,526 fans at Ebbets field, only 10,000 more than in 1946, National League attendance jumped by nearly 1.4 million. Robinson was partially the reason, as the Dodgers became the biggest draw in the National League and, for the first time, black fans began to attend Major League Baseball games in sizable numbers.

The Negro Leagues eventually paid the price. Beginning in 1947, attendance and interest in the Negro Leagues within the black community waned. Each time another black star signed a major league contract, interest in black baseball declined. Within a decade, the Negro Leagues were dead.

Robinson did not mourn their demise. He saw the existence of Negro League baseball as an impediment to the larger cause of integration and as a symbol of black exploitation by white owners. Neither he nor anyone else could yet foresee that the demise of the Negro Leagues, coupled with other changes in American society and foot-dragging by Major League Baseball's establishment, would ultimately result in a diminishing pool of black talent.

In an interview eight years ago, former *Boston Chronicle* Sports Editor Mabrey "Doc" Kountze, said that "by the time most teams got around to looking for black players, they were gone. The younger guys noticed how slow baseball was moving, and they stopped playing." Organized baseball simply failed to act quickly enough to fill the void the Negro Leagues left behind.

While Robinson was kept busy on the banquet circuit, Branch Rickey made good on a few promises he had made the year before, and reneged on a few others. On November 14, 1947, he sold Ed Stevens, who had a fine year at Montreal, to the Pittsburgh Pirates. On December 8 he packaged Dixie Walker and pitchers Hal Gregg and Vic Lombardi in another deal with Pittsburgh for pitcher Preacher Roe and infielders Billy Cox and Gene Mauch. The Boys of Summer were beginning to take shape.

Robinson traveled to Brooklyn in mid-February and signed a contract for the 1948 season for a reported $10,000. The Dodgers could afford it. Robinson had already earned them hundreds of thousands of dollars. By-in-large, many of the players who turned the Dodgers into a dynasty were acquired with the dollars the Dodgers earned off Robinson.

Jackie appeared before the press and admitted to being about fifteen pounds overweight, but didn't think he would have any trouble working off the weight. When asked if he would like to play second base, he diplomatically responded, "I don't see how anyone can push Eddie Stanky around. I feel I might be better at another position, but if they want me to play first, that's all right with me."

Three weeks later the only man who could push Stanky around did. On March 6, Rickey traded Stanky to the Boston Braves for second baseman Bama Rowell, first baseman Ray Sanders and cash. The door was open for Robinson to take over at second base.

Only Jackie was too big to fit through it.

In 1948 the Dodgers and Royals held spring training in Ciudad Trujillo in the Dominican Republic, once again choosing to not test the segregated South. The fact that President Trujillo paid the Dodgers $50,000 only made the arrangement sweeter to Rickey. Leo Durocher, his suspension over, resumed his job as manager.

Robinson attracted Durocher's ire from the first day of camp. He was two days late arriving from Hollywood after working out the details of his movie. He wasn't fifteen pounds overweight, but twenty-five. Jackie had hardly worked out all winter long.

Jackie and Branch Rickey sign another contract. (Transcendental Graphics)

Durocher took Robinson's portly appearance personally. He thought Jackie was trying to show him up. Leo was also eager to show the other Dodger players he was still the boss. His subsequent actions that spring in regard to Robinson and Roy Campanella may also have been designed to impress upon Rickey the fact that he, Durocher, had the final say on who played and who didn't. Durocher chose Robinson as his target.

Durocher disagreed with the Stanky trade, and when Robinson arrived out of shape, Durocher blasted him in the press and had Robinson work out at both second and first, although he didn't let him play second. In fact, Durocher hardly played him at all. He assigned coaches to run Robinson ragged chasing after ground balls and made him run in the outfield until Robinson thought he would drop. And unfortunately for Jackie, the pounds didn't melt off nearly as fast as he thought they would.

For the second year in a row, training camp was a mass of confusion. Robinson didn't appear at second base in a game until the third week of camp as Durocher gave Eddie Miksis a long look. Durocher wanted to make Campanella his catcher, but Rickey wanted Roy to spend at least part of the season integrating the American Association while playing for St. Paul. As the two fought, Campy played the outfield. Durocher also wanted to try rookie Gil Hodges at first. Rickey wanted him to stay behind the plate, so Pete Reiser was playing first. In addition, the Dodgers weren't even bothering to play other major league teams, rendering their undefeated record against minor league opponents meaningless.

It didn't help that Rickey decided to play another extended barnstorming season through the South, using Robinson to push integration in a number of cities. The club played in Fort Worth, Dallas, Oklahoma City and Tulsa, drawing huge crowds. Robinson agreed with Rickey's goal, but such trips were difficult for him as the

Jackie with Ruby Dee in The Jackie Robinson Story.

Within a few years Robinson became one of a handful of athletes to derive significant income from endorsements for products. (Transcendental Graphics)

Dodgers still left him to fend for himself. He usually stayed in a private home away from his teammates, ate separately, then performed under a microscope at the ballpark. Weakened by dieting and all those extra workouts, he played poorly. It was no way to prepare for the season.

Durocher finally started playing him at second, but kept pressuring Robinson to lose more weight. It didn't help when Robinson went hitless in the three-game series with the Yankees just before the start of the regular season.

The Dodgers opened the 1948 campaign with a 7-6 win over the Giants on April 20. Robinson played second and led off, but in the fifth inning of a 9-5 New York win the next day, Robinson was pulled from the lineup and benched in the fifth inning when he complained of a sore arm.

But Jackie wasn't out of the lineup long, and on May 2 he had one of the best offensive days of his career. In the first game of a double-header against Philadelphia, he tripled, homered and singled. In the early weeks of the season, Robinson was demonstrating some new-found power.

Durocher may have been pleased with Robinson's power, but that was the extent of his happiness. In mid-May he switched Robinson back to first base and made Miksis his second baseman.

In late May the Dodgers stunned everyone and asked for waivers on Robinson. In the administrative procedure, a team makes a player from the roster available for a nominal fee. If the player is claimed, the club can either let him go, or reassert their own claim.

The so-called "waiver wire" is used for a variety of reasons. Placing a player on waivers, for instance, can temporarily clear a roster spot. By paying attention to which clubs claim which players, a team can also get some idea of the needs of the competition, and use that information to make trades.

Still, asking waivers on Robinson was a shock,

Asking waivers of Jackie was a shock, even though it was mostly an administrative procedure. (National Baseball Library, Cooperstown, N.Y.)

Dodgers shortstop Pee Wee Reese (left) and Robinson execute a spring training double play. Both men were strong clubhouse leaders for the team and close friends off the field. (National Baseball Library, Cooperstown, N.Y.)

one Branch Rickey never adequately explained, later saying he used the strategy to fire up Robinson. The Dodgers were upset when the story was first made public, and even issued a denial.

Rickey may have been using Robinson to gauge the interest other NL clubs had in black players. Or he may have been serious about making a deal. Durocher and Robinson weren't getting along, and Leo wanted Campanella. Could the Dodgers play two blacks in their starting lineup? Rickey, too, was worried about Robinson's weight gain and may have been wondering just what Jackie would attract in trade.

Others have usually used the incident to mark a great turnaround for Robinson in a previously dismal year, but that is entirely inaccurate. He was already hitting over .300, and while he hadn't

stolen a base and wasn't in the best shape, he was among the league's RBI leaders and was back at second base, more or less permanently, by the end of the month.

The Dodgers meanwhile, got off to a slow start. Attendance lagged far behind their 1947 pace, and Rickey and Durocher were increasingly at odds over player personnel. By late May the Dodgers had fallen all way to last place and Dodgers Owners Walter O'Malley and John Smith were getting impatient. They blamed Durocher for the Dodgers poor showing at the gate. They wanted Rickey to fire him, but the Mahatma balked and was slow to act.

Durocher finally got Campanella, and when he did the club started winning, taking 16 of 19 to pull back into the pennant race. O'Malley and Smith were still adamant in their desire for

Jackie punctuated his 1948 season on August 29 when he hit for the cycle.   (National Baseball Library, Cooperstown, N.Y.)

Wherever he went, Jackie was popular with children. (International News Photo)

change. When the club lost six in a row just before the all-star break, Durocher was fired. Burt Shotton came back in his stead, and Durocher soon set up shop in Manhattan, as he was hired to manage the Giants.

The Dodgers played better under Shotton, and Robinson did get his legs in shape by August, when he started stealing bases again. On August 24 in Pittsburgh, he experienced a breakthrough. In the fourth inning, umpire Butch Henline called a strike on Gene Hermanksi. The Brooklyn bench went wild, and started hooting the umpire. He issued a warning, and when the catcalls failed to cease, Henline whirled around, ripped off his mask and pointed to the Brooklyn bench.

"You, Robinson!" he called out, "You're out of the game!" He had no trouble picking out Robinson's distinctive, high-pitched call from the chorus of voices. Robinson left the field without incident. He wasn't upset at being tossed from the game. As he later recalled, "That made me feel great. Henline didn't throw me out because I was black. He threw me out because I was getting on his nerves. It was wonderful to be treated like any other ballplayer."

Jackie punctuated his season on August 29. In the first game of a double-header sweep of the Cardinals, Robinson hit for the cycle, cracking a homer, triple, double and single in that order, stealing a base, scoring three runs and knocking in two. The sweep pulled the Dodgers into first place by percentage points.

Durocher's Giants swept a double-header from Brooklyn on September 4 to send them back to second place. Then, in a showdown series with the Braves, Boston came out on top to end the race. The Dodgers finished third at 84-70, 7 1/2 games back.

Robinson's year-end statistics mirrored those of his rookie season, although he nearly doubled his RBI total and collected the bulk of his 22 stolen bases in the last six weeks of the season. He performed well at second base, finishing second to Red Schoendienst in fielding, although Robinson, in his own autobiography, erroneously credits himself with leading the league. Despite his early troubles, he proved his rookie year was no fluke.

He took a job in the off-season at the Harlem YMCA, working with children, an assignment that also allowed him to keep in shape. He was determined to report to spring training in 1949 ready for the upcoming season.

In the off-season, the Dodgers built their own training facilities at Vero Beach, Florida, and the team finally held a camp that was something approaching normal. But for Robinson, the most important event of the year took place before camp. Branch Rickey lifted his strictures on Robinson's behavior. The battle over the integration of baseball had been won. There was no turning back, and Robinson no longer had to "turn the other cheek." Jackie gave warning to the National League that they would see a different Jackie Robinson in 1949. On the first day of spring training he told a reporter "They'd better be rough on me this year, because I'm going to be rough on them," a statement that caused Commissioner Happy Chandler to call on Robinson and make sure he didn't intend to start any battles. He assured the commissioner he did not, but if challenged by others, he intended to fight back.

The Dodgers annual barnstorming tour north was another excuse for Rickey to integrate baseball in a number of southern cities and ball parks, at the same time reaping the financial benefit. Nearly everywhere the Dodgers played they drew record crowds. There were few incidents, although in Atlanta Dr. Samuel Green, grand

dragon of the Ku Klux Klan, threatened to disrupt the Dodgers appearance before backing down and predicting their three-game set would be a failure.

Green could not have been more wrong. The three games in Atlanta drew over 50,000 fans, including six or seven thousand blacks at each game, who more than filled the sections of the park designated for their use and had to be put up in the outfield.

For once, the Dodgers began the regular season with something resembling a set lineup. Gil Hodges manned first, Billy Cox took over at third, Campanella caught and Duke Snider won the center field spot. On May 14 Don Newcombe was recalled from Montreal and became the third African-American on the squad. He solidified the rotation, and became the ace of the staff.

On the first day of the season the Dodgers served notice that they were a different ball club. Furillo, Robinson and Campanella all cracked home runs and the Dodgers dumped the Giants, 10-3, before an opening day record crowd of 34,530 at Ebbets Field. In addition to his home run, Robinson cracked out two other hits.

But after this quick start, Robinson cooled. Although he was once again the same whirling dervish on the base paths he had been in Montreal and was playing the best second base in the National League, he wasn't hitting. On May 1 his batting average was only .200. The Dodgers, at 7-6, were in fourth place.

The situation was only temporary. Shotton had installed Robinson in the cleanup spot in the batting order, and now it began to pay off. Robinson went on a tear, hitting over .400 for the month to push his average to .360. He was also hitting with power, and led the league with 38 RBIs. Moreover, his play carried the Dodgers into first place.

Jackie was doing everything—running the

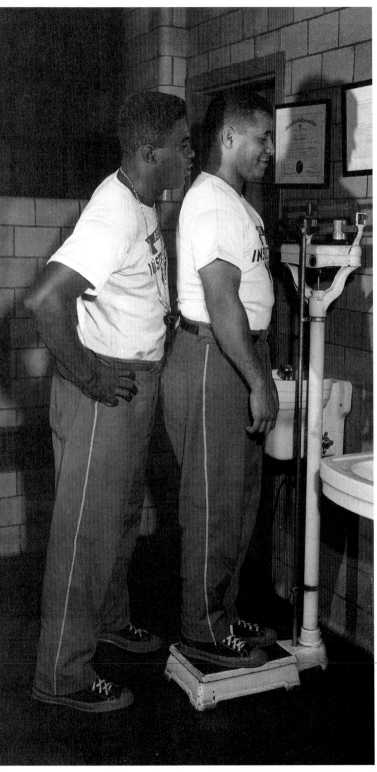

Robinson, shown here weighing in with teammate Roy Campanella, battled weight problems his entire career.
(Transcendental Graphics)

bases aggressively, stealing, worrying pitchers into making mistakes and slamming the ball all over the National League. Batting Robinson cleanup gave the Dodgers a unique advantage. When they failed to get a base runner in the first inning, Robinson led off the second, where he could use his speed to act as a second lead off man. It was unorthodox, but it worked.

Robinson was also standing up for himself with increasing regularity. Some observers had difficulty with the new Robinson. Where they had been sympathetic to Robinson the martyr, they found the new brash and bold Robinson disquieting. He regularly challenged umpires on close calls, slid into second just as hard as other players slid into him, and demonstrated he had learned a thing or two about applying the needle to opposing players.

The people that really mattered, the fans, accepted him. For the first time he was voted into the starting lineup in the all-star game, where he was joined by both Newcombe and Campanella, who were added to the squad by Boston Manager Billy Southworth. The game was played on July 12 at Ebbets Field.

The AL jumped out to a 4-0 lead in the top of the first. In the bottom half of the inning, Robinson, hitting second after Reese, doubled to left and scored on Musial's home run to make the score 4-2.

Robinson scored the NL's third run in the third. He led off with a walk, moved to third on Musial's base hit, and scored when Ralph Kiner hit into a double play. Jackie flew out in the fifth, but reached base a third time in the sixth on a fielder's choice and scored when Kiner homered. The AL won, 11-7.

Robinson was becoming important for more than what he did on the baseball field. He was, quite simply, the most visible black face in America. Increasingly, he was being called upon to serve as a spokesman.

Whether scoring a run or turning two, Jackie Robinson was the most exciting player on the field.
(National Baseball Library, Cooperstown, N.Y.)

For years Robinson contended that National League umpires allowed pitchers to brush him back with impunity. Here, Jackie is seen "discussing" a baserunning out. (Bettmann Archives)

Robinson's batting skill is probably the most underrated aspect of his career. (National Baseball Library, Cooperstown, N.Y.)

After Robinson was first signed by Rickey, he had been investigated by the House Un-American Activities Committee. In their zealous efforts to stifle discontent, they investigated thousands of Americans to ferret out any leftist leanings. The Committee likely uncovered some past association in Robinson's background they found troublesome, perhaps stemming from the 1942 "tryout" for the White Sox. But HUAC didn't want to expose Robinson, they wanted to use him. After protracted negotiations, Robinson agreed to "voluntarily" appear before the group.

In 1949, African-American singer, actor and political activist Paul Robeson gave a speech in Paris praising the Soviet Union. HUAC wanted to silence Robeson, and they chose Jackie Robinson to do so. Jackie was in an awkward spot, but in no real position to turn the committee down. With the help of Lester Granger, national director of the Urban League, he fash-

ioned a cautious statement on the relationship of American blacks to communism, and his own reaction to Robeson's statements.

Speaking before the committee, Robinson said, "Every single Negro who is worth his salt is going to resent any kind of slurs and discrimination because of his race . . . This has absolutely nothing to do with what the Communists may or may not be trying to do." At the end of his statement, he finally got around to Robeson. "I have been asked to express my views on Paul Robeson's statement in Paris to the effect that American Negroes would refuse to fight any war against Russia because we love Russia so much. I haven't any comment to make on that statement except that if Mr. Robeson actually made it, it sounds very silly to me."

Robinson's docile denunciation was front page news. He was widely praised in the mainstream press and the speech added to his popularity in white America. The scene was added to the upcoming movie version of his life.

It also foreshadowed the uncomfortable part politics would play in Robinson's later life. He was sensitive to his unique position in American society and tried to fulfill his political role. But just as it was not in Robinson's nature to turn the other cheek, neither was it in his nature to play either the role of diplomat or activist. He was an athlete, first and foremost, one whose achievements were earned at long odds through individual effort. Performing on the baseball field as an example for his race was one thing. Speaking out for others was an entirely different matter.

The public role never fit him comfortably, and most of his later activities are marked by a certain awkwardness and uncertainty. Years later, when the role of HUAC became more clear, Robinson came to realize he had been used and regretted his betrayal.

On the baseball field in 1949 he knew no such discomfort. He continued his stellar play after the all-star break as the Dodgers and St. Louis Cardinals left the rest of the league behind and battled each other for the National League pennant.

The match-up was appropriate. Robinson had not forgotten the rough play that marked his earlier appearances against the Cardinals. The two clubs were evenly matched. Each was led by a player—Robinson of the Dodgers and Musial of the Cardinals—who was clearly one of the best players in the league.

The Dodgers held the lead until July 24, when St. Louis won three straight in Brooklyn to pull ahead. Once the Cardinal's reached first place, they grimly held on, giving it up for only three days in mid-August before resuming control.

The Dodgers kept pace. Robinson was slowed by a tendon injury but kept playing. The team

Robinson dances to avoid a pitch in a game against the Boston Braves in 1953. (National Baseball Library, Cooperstown, N.Y.)

Robinson brought the inspiring style of play which he learned in the Negro Leagues to the majors. In this sequence from a game against the Cubs on May 23, 1953, Robinson dashes for third after a pickoff throw from Johnny Schmitz eludes Wayne Terwilliger. Such aggresive play was characteristic of Robinson.
(Associated Press National Baseball Library, Cooperstown, N.Y.)

Jackie met Rachel, his future bride, while they were students at UCLA. This photo was taken in 1949, three years after their marriage, outside of where Jackie testified before the House Un-American Affairs Committee, (Acme Photo, National Baseball Library, Cooperstown, N.Y.)

Don Newcombe squared off in a classic pitcher's duel. Entering the ninth inning, each pitcher was working on a five-hit shutout.

Brooklyn went quietly in the bottom of the inning. In the Cardinal half, Robinson's nemesis, Enos Slaughter, led off.

Slaughter and Robinson had more in common than the earlier spiking incident. The two were in a pitched battle for the NL batting title. Entering the game, Robinson led by four points. Slaughter had robbed him of a hit earlier in the game. Entering the ninth, both men were hitless.

Then Slaughter drew close. Newcombe had him 0-2 and threw a third pitch knee-high over the heart of the plate. Umpire Bill Stewart called the pitch a ball and the Dodgers howled. When Newcombe finally settled down, he threw another nasty pitch low and away to Slaughter. The veteran hitter went with the pitch and sliced a fly ball that kicked up chalk in left field for a double. From second base, Robinson continued to berate Stewart.

Newcombe then walked Bill Northey to set up the double play. Cardinal center fielder Bill Howerton responded by dropping a bunt down the third base line.

At third, Eddie Miksis watched as the ball rolled toward the foul line then straightened and stayed fair. The bases were loaded.

Coach Clyde Sukeforth raced out from the Dodgers bench to calm Newcombe. Robinson joined the conference, and as Sukeforth trotted off and Jackie turned to go back to second, he got umpire Stewart's attention and grabbed his own throat in the classic "choke" sign.

Stewart flew out from behind the plate with his thumb in the air and tossed Robinson from the game. The two squared off and jawed at each other some more, but Robinson walked off the field.

The Dodgers switched up, moving Miksis to second and bringing in Jorgenson at third. The

needed him. As August turned into September, the Dodgers matched the Cardinals win-by-win and loss-by-loss, never falling more than 2 1/2 games behind, yet never quite catching St. Louis either.

The season came down to the final ten days. The Dodgers rolled into St. Louis on September 21 off a three-game sweep of the Cubs, all shutouts, trailing the Cardinals by 1 1/2 games with only nine left to play.

The two played a unique "split" double-header, one game in the afternoon and the other at night so St. Louis could maximize the gate. In the first game, Cardinal pitcher Max Lanier and next hitter, Joe Garagiola, hit the ball sharply to second, where it took a big hop and went over Miksis' shoulder. Final score, 1-0 St. Louis. The Dodgers trailed by 2 1/2.

The night game was a must win for the Dodgers. They did. Preacher Roe hurled a shutout and Brooklyn pushed across five runs in the fourth inning to win, 5-0. They were right back where they had started. Robinson went hitless for the day and now trailed Slaughter, who had three hits, by four points in the batting race.

Brooklyn closed to within a half game the next day as their offense got untracked. They blasted six Cardinal pitchers for nineteen hits in the 19-6 win. Carl Furillo went 5-for-6 and had seven RBIs. Robinson's two hits put him one point ahead of Slaughter.

The Dodgers returned to Brooklyn on September 24 and beat the Phillies while the Cardinals defeated the Cubs. The next day, the Dodgers blew a chance to win when Robinson,

Robinson testified before the House Un-American Affairs Committee in 1949 to chastise Paul Robeson for statements the performer had made relative to African-Americans and Soviet Communism. (Courtesy of The Boston Herald)

playing aggressively, made two base running gaffs. In the fourth, he ran up Carl Furillo's back at third when Furillo was held up trying to score from second on a single. In the seventh, after doubling and stealing third, Jackie was picked off by catcher Andy Seminick. The Dodgers lost, 5-3, while the Cards won to go back up by one-and-a-half games.

Then St. Louis slumped. When the Dodgers swept Boston on September 29 and the Cards lost their third straight, Brooklyn pulled into the lead by one-half game. The Dodgers went into Philadelphia for the final two games of the season while St. Louis played the Cubs in Chicago. On the first day, Brooklyn blew a chance to clinch by losing to the Phillies 6-4 while St. Louis lost to the Cubs 3-1.

The season came down to the final day, with Don Newcombe squaring off against Philadelphia's Russ Meyer. Both pitchers were 17-8.

After two scoreless innings, Spider Jorgenson singled sharply with one out in the third, moved to second on a wild pitch and advanced to third on Duke Snider's force out.

Robinson came to plate. He turned on a pitch and bounced it toward third. Willie Jones, the Phillies third baseman, was playing in. Even with two outs he had to protect against the bunt. The ball bounced over his head and Jorgenson scored to give the Dodgers the lead. Jackie immediately stole second and moved to third on a wild pitch. Furillo beat out a hit to the hole and Robinson scored. The Dodgers ended the inning up 5-0.

But Newcombe wasn't equal to the task. In the fourth, the Phillies scored four times to chase the big pitcher. The Dodgers came back in the top of the fifth to score twice on a Campanella double, but Philadelphia came back with three more runs in the fifth and sixth off Rex Barney to tie the game 7-7.

In the seventh, the Phillies pulled out all the

Branch Rickey (center) holds court at Yankee Stadium on October 4, 1949 prior to the start of the World Series with (l-r) Gil Hodges, Gene Hermanski and Robinson. (Courtesy of The Boston Herald)

Prior to the 1949 World Series, Jackie meets with teammates Roy Campanella and Don Newcombe. (Associated Press)

Dodgers Manager Burt Shotton (left), shown with Casey Stengel prior to the 1949 World Series, took over from Clyde Sukeforth after one game and led the Dodgers to their first pennant since 1941.
(Courtesy of The Boston Herald)

stops, bringing in ace starter, left-handed Ken Heintzelman. At the end of nine, the score was still tied. Meanwhile, the Cards were routing the Cubs on their way to an eventual 13-5 win. A Dodgers loss would result in a play off with St. Louis.

Pee Wee Reese opened the tenth with a single to left. Miksis bunted him to second. Snider, who had trouble with left-handed pitching, then fought off a tough pitch and smacked it up the middle. Reese ran hard the whole way and just beat Richie Ashburn's throw to the plate to give the Dodgers the lead as Snider took second.

With Robinson at bat, Heintzelman walked him intentionally, then gave way to reliever Ken Trinkle. Luis Olmo singled in Snider with the insurance run. Pitcher Jack Banta held on, and the Dodgers won the pennant by a single game.

Meanwhile in the Bronx, the Yankees beat Boston 5-3 to likewise win the American League

pennant on the season's final day. The World Series would be a rematch of 1947.

Robinson's single in the season's final game gave him the batting title over Slaughter, .342 to .336. Robinson also led the league with 37 stolen bases, the most in the NL since the Cubs KiKi Cuyler swiped the same number in 1930. His 124 RBIs trailed only Ralph Kiner, his 203 hits were second best to Musial, his 122 runs scored were third best to Reese and Musial. He added 16 home runs, played in every game, had the fourth highest slugging percentage in the league and was now considered perhaps the best fielding second baseman in the game. It was a tour de force performance, one of the best all-around exhibitions in the history of the game to that time.

But the Dodgers just couldn't crack the Yankees. Allie Reynolds spun a two-hitter to best Don Newcombe's five-hit effort in Game One to

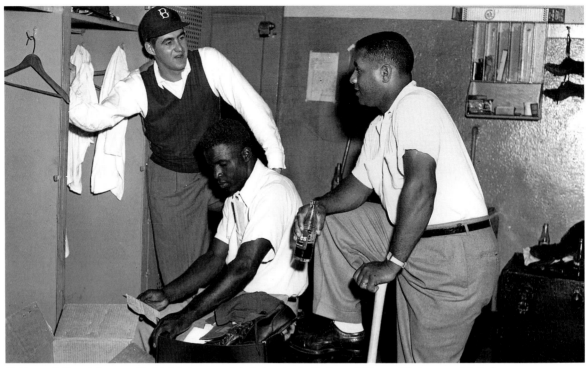

Robinson (left) and Campanella (right) clean out their lockers in the Dodgers clubhouse follwing one of their few non pennant winning seasons in 1948. (Transcendental Graphics)

win 1-0. In Game Two, it was Preacher Roe's turn to twirl a shutout, as he beat Vic Raschi by the identical score. Robinson scored the game's only run and Brooklyn's first of the series with a first-inning double. He moved to third on a fly ball and scored on Hodges single.

The Yankees won the next three games, 4-3, 6-4 and 10-6 to win the title.

Apart from the Game-Two double, Robinson was nearly shut down. For the Series, he collected only three hits and walked four times, but failed to steal a base and scored only twice.

Jackie's disappointing showing did little to dim the luster of this regular season performance. Most agreed with sports writer Tom Meany, who earlier that year asked "Who would you pick as the most dangerous player in baseball today? Stan Musial? Ted Williams? Let's not kid ourselves, fellows, the most dangerous player in baseball today is . . . Jackie Robinson [who] can beat you more ways than any other player in baseball today."

Indeed, Robinson out-polled the Cardinal's Stan Musial, and was voted the Most Valuable Player in the National League.

Another barrier had just fallen.

Visible Man

by Luke Salisbury

It is impossible to imagine the landscape of baseball without Brooklyn, and it is impossible to imagine Brooklyn without Jackie Robinson. Both are gone. Brooklyn no longer has a baseball team and no athlete is a pioneer for a great cause. The phrase Brooklyn Dodgers survives as a testament to the poetic qualities of language and our need for myth.

The Brooklyn myth, and the myth of New York City in the 1940s and '50s is the self-congratulatory, nostalgic stuff of cultural memory. Brooklyn in the age of Jackie Robinson is the golden age of the urban white working class. This city wasn't "inner" and full of despair, but "teeming with life," and European immigrants and their children, who dreamed the American dream, learned English, fought the Good War, worked hard, and loved baseball like the American flag. The reward for keeping faith was doing well enough to get out of Brooklyn, move to the suburbs, and venerate the Dodgers. This Brooklyn is a time when America worked, cities were safe, and if you melted in the pot, you got a share of the Dream.

Jackie Robinson and the Dodgers are the jewel of the myth. Robinson's breaking the twentieth century color line and the wonderful teams he played for, ever pitted against the gray flannel perfection of the Yankees in the World Series, bitterly fighting the cross-town Giants on beer-filled summer nights, superhumanly turning the other cheek to the race-baiting of Ben Chapman and the Phillies and the constant stream of racist abuse from every dugout and the stands of every park, is the very stuff of heroism. We like to think if we'd been there, we would have rooted for Jackie and demanded bigots be silent.

Brooklyn is a comfortable myth, especially if you don't live in a city. As to how we would have reacted in 1947, a better question might be, when was the last time a person of color ate at your house? When was the last time you talked on the phone to a person of color that wasn't business? Do you have Black neighbors? That we may not have come as far as we like to think is not Jackie Robinson's fault, but provides a clue to what he was up against not just in '47, but his whole life.

Emerson said, "The secret of the world is the tie between person and event," and Jackie Robinson's story is the story of one man in the most visible position any person of color had been allowed since Frederick Douglas. It's almost impossible to imagine the complete and total segregation of American society before the Second World War. In the Velvet Corridor of Georgia, near Albany, where Robinson was born in 1919, the sharecropping conditions of Black farmers were poverty at its most grinding and desperate. After his father abandoned them, Jackie's mother, a strong and deeply religious woman, moved the family to Pasadena, California, where she worked as a domestic to support five children. Pasadena provided another kind of education. The Robinsons lived on an all-white street and were jeered. The children went to almost all-white schools and were the first punished. Jackie was a member of the Pepper Street gang and stole. Friends remember he like to start trouble, especially in the segregated movie houses where he would often sit in the white section. Jackie liked to throw firecrackers at his buddies and "ride" smaller kids. He later said his mother and sports kept him out of reform school. Track sent his brother Mack to Pasadena Junior College and Oregon. Jackie followed and outdid him. At UCLA Jackie was a football star, a terrific basketball player (a sport whose difficulty and beauty weren't appreciated), a track star and played shortstop for the baseball team. Jackie quit before getting a degree, telling his future wife he didn't think it mattered much.

The young Robinson was intelligent, angry, and extraordinarily athletically gifted. He was an officer in the segregated US Army, where an incident on a Southern bus—Jackie wouldn't go to the back—led to a court marshal. He was exonerated and given a technically honorable discharge. Robinson had been trying to get doctors to exempt him from combat on the basis of an old football injury. Perhaps his reaction to the world wasn't so different from Malcolm Little, later Malcolm X, who didn't want to fight for the white man either. Five years later, when Jackie Robinson was the most important person of color in America, he was bullied into denouncing Paul Robeson in front of the House of Un-American Activities Committee.

What makes Robinson's story so interesting is the real Jack Robinson is not the Christ-like figure he portrayed in the movie The Jackie Robinson Story. He is more interesting and more remarkable. Jackie Robinson was an angry man. He was a man who fought when challenged. He was distrustful of white people and had no illusions about his future as a Blackman in America.

In 1947, when the racial melting of major league baseball began, Mr. Jack Robinson was put in the most difficult position an athlete has ever been in. He didn't simply have to perform, and hold back the anger and fury built over a lifetime of slights, insults, the mammoth and universal racial unfairness of America, he had to perform knowing exactly how much the "experiment" meant to every Black person in America, which was everything.

Baseball was the center stage of American popular culture in 1947. It was more important than Hollywood which presented the Blackman as stereotype, good or bad. Baseball was more visible than the stage or opera or writing a book or singing at the Lincoln Memorial. Major league baseball was the most visible, level or not, playing field in America. If Blackmen could play on it, Black people could do anything: go to school with whites, work with whites, even, though it was unthinkable in 1947, marry and live in neighborhoods of their choosing.

The way Robinson played was equally important. He brought back the in-your-face style of Ty Cobb. Indeed, in a remark of inexhaustible irony, Bill "Bojangles" Robinson, the great dancer and no relation, called Jackie "Ty Cobb in Technicolor." The style—dancing off the bases to drive a pitcher nuts, stealing home, scoring from 2nd on an infield hit, relentlessly intimidating and baiting, was Negro League baseball. In the white game it was revolutionary. Jackie Robinson was "uppity" and had to be. He was in America's face and we are so much the better for it. Jackie Robinson was Black energy making its way, however slowly, however obliquely, into the American mainstream. When this energy hit music, the result was rock and roll. In basketball and football, we got the modern game. In literature, Ralph Ellison and James Baldwin. In politics, we are waiting.

Jackie Robinson playing for the Brooklyn Dodgers was the most important symbolic American event of the twentieth century. Branch Rickey somehow picked a man who could tame himself, survive indescribable pressure, play at a Hall of Fame level, and give us one of our most cherished myths. I'm not sure any American, not even Martin Luther King, went through what Robinson went through. The secret of the tie between Jackie Robinson and his events is not just that anyone can make it, but that America might make it.

Luke Salisbury is a Professor of Communications at Bunker Hill Community College in Charlestown, Massachusetts where he teaches Film, American Studies, and English. He is the author of *The Answer is Baseball* and the novels *The Cleveland Indian and Blue Eden.* His essays have appeared in biographies of Ted Williams and Joe DiMaggio by Glenn Stout and Dick Johnson as well as in publications such as *The Boston Globe, Spitball, Nine, Fan, SABR Review of Books, AERA* (Japan), and many others. He is past Vice President and National Secretary of the Society for American Baseball Research.

THE PLAYER:
1950-1953

The word "player" in the Most Valuable Player award makes an interesting distinction in regard to Robinson. In many ways that is just what he became in 1949, another player, albeit a most valuable one. Racial tensions on the Dodgers club virtually ceased. Several players, among them his middle infield partner Pee Wee Reese, were now truly friendly. At worst, they considered him just another teammate, and everyone knew just what he meant to the Dodgers team.

Jackie still had trouble with a few players around the league, but even those conflicts were starting to abate and take on the character of usual tussles between opponents in the heat of competition. His was not the only black face in the major leagues. By the end of the 1949 season, eight other African-Americans had followed in Robinson's wake. While not all made the grade, it was now more or less accepted that African-Americans were in the major leagues for good, even if most franchises had yet to take the final step.

Jackie Robinson, after three long seasons, was at last a player.

His play in 1949 got the Dodgers attention. Not only was he one of the best players in the game, he was a team leader. While Reese captained the club, Robinson was the guy everyone looked toward to provide the big hit. Only a few players remained from the team Robinson joined in 1947, and he was now a veteran, the third oldest player on the team. The club rewarded him with a contract for 1950 worth $45,000, the highest of his career.

His daughter, Sharon, was born on January 13. After the birth, Jackie raced to Hollywood and began filming his life story, in which he played the starring role.

Filming under a tight schedule and an even tighter budget, *The Jackie Robinson Story* was released later that year to mostly kind reviews. As soon as filming was complete, Jackie dashed off to spring training.

Led once more by Robinson, the 1950 Dodgers again boasted of a powerful starting lineup and Brooklyn's bats kept them in the pennant race. In mid-season, Brooklyn, St. Louis, Philadelphia and Boston all appeared poised to make the NL pennant race another Darwinian, survival-of-the-fittest contest.

Robinson never hit better than in the first half of the 1950 season, although his ankle, which he severely sprained during camp, kept him from running as much as in the past. On July 1 he led the league with a .371 batting average and 53 runs scored. If there was an MVP at mid-season, it was Jackie. He was again voted to the all-star

team, and his 1,061,522 votes paced the National League.

The Dodgers offense was not enough. Pitching, particularly relief pitching, was Brooklyn's downfall. Time and time again the Dodgers slugged their way to an early lead only to lose when the bullpen collapsed. Shotton tried everyone on the staff in relief, but his manipulations did no good.

Led by Robin Roberts, Curt Simmons and an MVP performance by relief man Jim Konstanty, the Phillies had the pitching Brooklyn lacked. Entering September, the Dodgers trailed by more than ten games. Brooklyn appeared to be out of the race.

And there were other distractions.

In mid-July, Dodgers Co-Owner John L. Smith died, precipitating a pitched battle for control of the club between Walter O'Malley and Branch Rickey. Smith had usually sided with Rickey, allowing him to run the club without

Jackie won the George Washington Carver award for outstanding contributions to the betterment of racial relations in 1949. Here he is flanked by Baseball Commissioner Happy Chandler at left and publisher Frank Gannett at right.
(International News Photo)

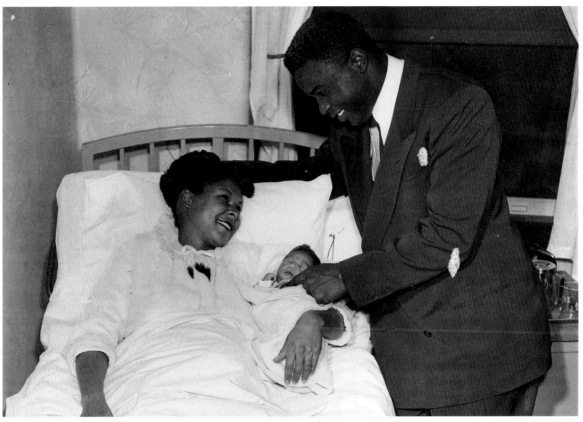

The Robinson family welcomed a new addition, Sharon, in January 1950. (Transcendental Graphics)

interference. Now O'Malley was able to gain control. Rickey's days were numbered.

The situation worried Jackie. O'Malley made no bones about his personal dislike of Robinson and his special relationship with Rickey, calling him "Rickey's prima donna." On August 12 in Boston, Robinson made an off-the-cuff comment in regard to the battle between Rickey and O'Malley. "It wouldn't surprise me," he said, "if I were traded." A few days later Jackie added to the controversy. "Actually I have no idea whether they intend to trade me or not . . . However, I'm prepared for anything that may happen . . . I'd hate to leave Brooklyn, though."

His comment drew a response from Rickey, who had yet to admit he was on the losing end of his battle with O'Malley. "I haven't given a thought to trading Robinson or any other player," he said. "Of course I don't mean that Robinson

can't be had for any price," he added, "If I were offered two ball clubs for him I would consider trading Jackie."

As if in response to a call from their deposed creator, the team's pitching finally started to improve and Brooklyn surged. Philadelphia stumbled when Curt Simmons entered the service. On September 24 Brooklyn pulled to within seven games and arrived in Philadelphia for a critical series.

In the first game of the series, Robinson opened the second inning with a single. Furillo followed with another base hit, then Gil Hodges blasted a home run into the left field stands of Philadelphia's Shibe Park. Don Newcombe went the distance and hung on for a 3-2 win. The Dodgers drew closer the next day with a 11-0 win behind twenty-two-year-old pitcher Erv Palica. Robinson, who had been in and out of the lineup

National League President Ford Frick presents Jackie with the Silver Bat Award after Jackie won the batting title in 1949.

(Bettmann Archives)

Robinson, nursing his sore thumb, takes in a game as a spectator with son Jackie Jr. on September 10, 1950.

(Transcendental Graphics)

Robinson's increasing fame led to a fifteen minute television show entitled, Jackie Robinson's Sports Classroom *on WPIX which debuted on Prime Time (7:15 p.m.) on December 14, 1950.* (Transcendental Graphics)

Ebbets Field was the scene of Robinson's All-Star Game debut in 1949, which also coincided with the All-Star debuts of fellow African-Americans Larry Doby, Roy Campanella and Don Newcombe. Robinson is shown here with teammate Pee Wee Reese and Giants Johnny Mize (left) and Willard Marshall (right). (Courtesy of The Boston Herald)

His hair flecked with gray, Robinson had aged perceptably and was slower by half a step on the basepaths by 1953. Here he is tagged out by Giants third baseman Hank Thompson in a game at the Polo Grounds in August, 1953. (Bettmann Archives)

due to injuries, led the charge with his first home run in a month.

The defeats shook the Phillies, who dropped both ends of two double-headers to the Giants while the Dodgers took three of four against Boston. With two days remaining in the season, the Phillies came to Brooklyn.

Palica shined again in the first game, beating the Phillies 7-3. The two teams met on October 1 to decide the pennant. Newcombe faced Roberts in a match-up of pitching greats. For five innings, both proved they were the best, as neither allowed the opposing team to even entertain the thought of scoring.

In the sixth, with two out, Dick Sisler rolled a ground ball through the right side for a hit. Then Del Ennis popped the ball into short center. Robinson ranged back, but appeared to pull up as center fielder Duke Snider raced in. But Snider, playing Ennis deep, couldn't reach the ball. It fell for a hit and Sisler made third. He scored on Willie Jones' base hit to put the Phillies up, 1-0.

The Dodgers got the run back in their half of the inning when Reese popped a high fly down the right field line. In almost any other ballpark in America, the ball was an easy out, but at Ebbets Field, it was only 275 feet down the line. The nineteen-foot-high concrete wall was topped by a nineteen-foot-high wire fence, and Reese's ball cleared the first obstacle but failed to make it over the second. The hit scraped the screen, landed on top of the wall, bounced a few times—and stayed there. Reese raced around the bases for the most unlikely of all inside-the-park home runs to tie the score.

But the play used up all the Brooklyn luck. They blew a chance to score in the ninth when Cal Abrams was thrown out at the plate with no outs and, after an intentional walk to Robinson loaded the bases, Furillo popped up and Hodges flew out. Dick Sisler of the Phillies cracked a

Despite the disappointment of a near miss in the pennant race, Robinson had a superb season in 1950, batting .328.
(National Baseball Library, Cooperstown, N.Y.)

three-run homer in the top of the tenth to win the game, and the pennant, for Philadelphia.

A disconsolate Robinson sat a long time in the clubhouse after the game. He had gone hitless, and his failure to catch Ennis' pop had proved critical. He was tired, sore, and uncertain of his future in Brooklyn. Bothered by a series of nagging injuries in the second half, he had slumped from his strong start to finish with an average of .328. He was down in most other categories, as well, and managed to steal only 12 bases.

On October 28, 1950, Branch Rickey introduced Walter O'Malley as the new Dodgers president. Rickey was out.

O'Malley set out to purge Rickey's memory from the Dodgers front office. Montreal General Manager Buzzy Bavasi was brought in to handle

On July 7, 1950 National League President Ford Frick presented Robinson with his 1949 National League MVP plaque in a ceremony at Ebbets Field. (National Baseball Library, Cooperstown, N.Y.)

Rickey's personnel duties. Mere mention of Rickey's name in the front office drew a one dollar fine. Rickey moved on to assume charge of the Pittsburgh Pirates.

The new Dodgers president made few changes, save one. He replaced Burt Shotton with Charley Dressen.

For the first two-thirds of the 1951 season O'Malley was in his glory because his Dodgers were doing something Branch Rickey's Dodgers never did: they were running away with the pennant.

The changes were mostly semantic, for the 1951 Dodgers were the same ballclub Rickey had put together. But they were playing better. Of that, there was no doubt.

The troubles with relief pitching disappeared, not because anyone suddenly stepped to the fore, but because the starting pitching was so good the relievers were rarely needed. Preacher Roe had the best season of his career, Newcombe was nearly as good, while Branca and Carl Erskine were the best third and fourth starters in the league. The Dodger lineup was just as powerful as the year before, and Robinson, playing injury-free, was still hitting and finally able to run again with something approaching his usual abandon.

The only malfunction in the Dodgers machine centered around Robinson. As the Dodgers blasted the Giants in five out of six games in April to move into first place and send New York to the cellar, and Robinson was smacking out eight RBIs to make it so, Jackie and the Giants went after each other.

It began with a spat between Robinson and Giants pitcher Larry Jansen, which precipitated a beanball war as Durocher tried to put Jackie in his place. In the final game of the series, the Giants first win after eleven consecutive losses, Robinson took matters into his own hands by dropping a bunt down the third base line and running over Giant pitcher Sal Maglie.

Durocher called it "a bush stunt." Robinson responded testily, "If it's a bush stunt he's a bush manager. He taught me how to do it." The incident eventually led to an exchange between Robinson and NL president Ford Frick. Robinson charged that league umpires allowed pitchers to throw at him with impunity. "I'm willing to take it as long as I can give it back," he fumed. Frick told the Dodgers, "if they can't control Robinson, I will." Jackie steamed, but kept himself more or less in check for the remainder of the season, although he still went after umpires regularly.

Meanwhile, all the Dodgers did was win. On August 12, the Dodgers led the second place Giants by 13 1/2 games. Robinson's .344 average was much of the reason. Although the Giants were in many ways the Dodgers equal, the early losing streak appeared to have knocked them from the pennant race.

The rest of the season is etched in the hearts and minds of Dodgers and Giants fans with a

Robinson leads the "Boys of Summer" in an Ebbets Field rhubarb. (Bettmann Archives)

Hall of Famer Monte Irvin of the Giants was another Negro League veteran who successfully followed in Robinson's footsteps.

clarity that has not dimmed in the ensuing forty-five seasons. Brooklyn went into the Polo Grounds on August 15 with a chance to bury the Giants for good, while New York, winners of their last three, saw the series as their last chance to make a pennant race.

The Giants won all three hard-fought contests, 4-2, 3-1 and 2-1. Significantly, Robinson was forced out of the first game with leg trouble, replaced by Wayne Terwilliger, and missed game two entirely. He returned for the third game, even beating out an infield hit, but the Dodgers were further hampered when Pee Wee Reese was forced to play with a charley horse. His backup, Rocky Bridges, had hurt his hand in the first game of the set.

The suddenly battered Dodgers now led the Giants by only 9 1/2. The Giants went on to win their next ten games, for a total of sixteen in a row. By September 1, when Brooklyn came to the Polo Grounds for a two-game set, they led by only seven.

Brooklyn slunk out with a five-game lead, as the Giants won twice. The first game, an 8-1 defeat of Branca by Maglie, was marked by the resumption of the bean ball war. With the Giants leading, Robinson came up with the bases loaded and was hit by Maglie.

The umpire summoned management of both teams and warned them not to retaliate, but over the next six innings Whitey Lockman of the Giants was hit twice, while Monte Irvin, Willie Mays and Roy Campanella were all sent sprawling.

New York kept up the pressure all through September. On the 25th, they beat the Phillies while the Dodgers dropped two in Boston to close to within a game. In the first inning of the second game, Robinson was hit squarely in the chest by a pitch thrown by Jim Wilson of the Braves. He stayed in until the fourth, then left complaining of dizziness. Doctors worried that he'd bruised his heart.

Jackie proved there was nothing wrong with his heart the next day, as Brooklyn blasted the Braves 15-5. Robinson punctuated the win by stealing home in the seventh off Lew Burdette.

The Giants refused to lose as the Dodgers kept stumbling, falling again to the Braves as New York had an off day, then losing to Philadelphia while the Giants enjoyed a second day off. The race was tied. On September 29, with only two games left, Don Newcombe shut out Philadelphia while Maglie blanked Boston. Going into the final day, both clubs had identical 95-58 records.

Dressen brought Preacher Roe back on two-days rest to face Bubba Church. He didn't last the second inning as the Phillies jumped ahead, 4-0. In the third, the Dodgers got one run back on Reese's triple, then Philadelphia scored twice more off Ralph Branca to lead 6-1. It looked good for the Giants, who were on their way to beating Boston, 3-2, but the Dodgers cut the lead to four with a single run in the fourth. Then in the fifth, Furillo and Reese singled.

Robinson was up. He drove a Church pitch hard to right, knocking in both men as he charged around the bases for a triple. Andy Pafko knocked him home with a single off reliever Karl Drews to make the score 6-5. However, the Phillies weren't through. They scored twice in the bottom of the inning to increase their lead to 8-5.

In Boston, the Giants won and were getting ready to leave Braves Field for the train station when a radio reporter entered the clubhouse anxious to get some quotes from the Giants celebrating the pennant. One player allegedly turned to him and said of the Dodgers-Phillies game, "Robinson is there—anything can happen."

Anything did. The Dodgers came back. Hodges and Billy Cox singled before Rube Walker cracked a pinch-hit double, scoring both. The Phillies, relishing the thought of dumping the Dodgers in the last game of the season for the second year in a row, brought Robin Roberts in to face Carl Furillo. He singled, and the game was tied at eight.

As the Giants train chugged toward New York, the score stayed tied as Newcombe came back on no days rest to shut down Philadelphia. Roberts did the same to the Dodgers. But in the twelfth, the Phillies threatened.

Newcombe walked Roberts, then threw too late to get the force on a sacrifice by second baseman Eddie Pellagrini. Ashburn hit into a force out and Willie Jones walked. Newcombe then struck out Del Ennis. Eddie Waitkus stepped to the plate with two outs and the bases loaded. He hit a rocket up the middle.

Robinson was the "lion in winter" during a glorious 1956 season which saw the Dodgers win the pennant on the final day of the season. He is shown scoring against the Braves on September 11th in a 4-2 Dodgers win. (Bettmann Archives)

The Dodgers dugout erupts at the Polo Grounds on October 2, 1951 as Robinson is greeted by teammates after hitting a two-run homer in the second inning of the second playoff game against the Giants. (Bettmann Archives)

As Harold Rosenthal wrote in the *Herald Tribune*, "Robinson simply had to make that catch and he made it. He flung himself at the ball, made a tumbling stop, and in so doing, jammed his elbow into his side."

Robinson stayed on the ground after the catch, wincing and rolling back and forth. It was five full minutes before he rose and left the field to polite and yet somewhat cheerful applause. Philly fans presumed he was out of the game.

He wasn't. After both teams went down in the thirteenth, Robinson came to bat against Roberts. Robin threw two pitches that Jackie took. With the count 1-1, he threw a fastball. Jackie swung and the ball soared into the upper deck in left field. Bud Podbielan held Philadelphia scoreless in the bottom of the fourteenth, and the Dodgers won, 9-8.

All that did was set up a three game playoff with the Giants, scheduled to begin the next day.

Without time to breathe, the Dodgers caught a train back to Brooklyn. As Red Smith wrote in his summation of the game, " . . . Then Robinson's home run and the finish. Brooklyn's still in the league. And the crowd is still in the ballpark. The season is over. But they won't go home."

The playoffs began in Brooklyn the following day. The Giants selected a well-rested Jim Hearn to start, while the Dodgers, their pitching worn thin, had little choice but to counter Ralph Branca, loser of five in a row.

Andy Pafko got Brooklyn on board first with a second-inning home run. But in the fourth Bobby Thomson smacked a two run homer and Monte Irvin added a final run in the eighth with a solo shot. The Giants won, 3-1, but Branca's eight strong innings gave the Dodgers staff a rest.

Clem Labine got the call for game two in the Polo Grounds. Sheldon Jones took the mound for the Giants. After the closest of all pennant races, game two was a rout. Reese singled in the first, and Robinson swung at the first pitch and drove the ball just over the left field fence for a home run and a 2-0 Dodgers lead. The Giants squandered several early chances, and after a sixth-inning rain delay, Brooklyn exploded, scoring eight times to win going away, 10-0.

After 156 games, the season came down to one final contest, Maglie versus Newcombe, in the Polo Grounds. If baseball ever disappears from the mind of America, this game is likely to be the last one remembered.

Maglie struggled early. In the first, he walked Reese and Snider before Robinson stepped up. For the third time in four days, when given the opportunity to put the Dodgers ahead, he delivered, driving a single to left to knock in Reese. The Dodgers led, 1-0.

Then Maglie and Newcombe settled into a pitcher's duel. The Giants tied it in the seventh when Irvin doubled, took third on a bunt, and scored on Bobby Thomson's sacrifice.

Brooklyn came back in the eighth. With one out, Reese singled. Snider followed with a hit and Reese took third. With Robinson up, Maglie worked carefully. He bounced a pitch past catcher Wes Westrum and Reese scored as Snider went all the way to third. Then Maglie walked Robinson to set up the double play.

Pinch hitter Andy Pafko grounded to third, but Thomson, on a roller coaster all day, couldn't come up with it. Snider scored as Jackie went to second. He came around on Cox's single to give the Dodgers a 4-1 lead.

It stayed that way into the ninth. The Dodgers failed to score.

All Newcombe needed were three outs. But

Dodgers Manager Charley Dressen congratulated Robinson following his heroics in the final game of the 1951 season. Robinson helped lead his team to 9-8 victory over the Phillies with a key catch and game winning home run in extra innings as the Dodgers earned the right to meet the Giants in a best of three game playoff for the 1951 National league pennant. (Associated Press, National Baseball Library, Cooperstown, N.Y.)

Former Dodgers Manager Leo Durocher, denied the opportunity to manage Robinson in 1947, became a father figure to a rookie named Willie Mays. (National Baseball Library, Cooperstown, N.Y.)

over the last five days, he had pitched twenty-two innings. He didn't have a twenty-third in the tank. Dark led off and singled just out of the reach of Hodges. Then Mueller singled, sending Dark to third.

Irvin popped out to Hodges in foul territory for the first out, but Lockman doubled to score Dark. Mueller slid safely into third, but sprained his ankle. There was a delay of several minutes before he was carried off the field, replaced by Clint Hartung.

Dressen replaced Newcombe with Branca, and Thomson stepped up for the Giants. Willie Mays was on deck. What happened next has been replayed in the mind's eye ever since. No one who was there or ever cared about those two teams nor anyone in the game will ever forget this moment.

As Rud Rennie wrote, "Branca's first pitch was a strike. His second was the end of the world for the Dodgers." Thomson stroked the high inside pitch into the lower left-field stands, sending radio broadcaster Russ Hodges apoplectic, hastening autumn into Brooklyn and leaving the Dodgers to sleepwalk off the field, stunned, their eyes vacant with disbelief.

As Thomson danced around the bases trailed by a growing string of ecstatic Giants fans, only one of the Dodgers stayed in the game. At second base, Jackie Robinson carefully watched Thomson's celebratory navigation of the bases. He stared intently as Thompson plunked his foot on each and kept his eyes trained on him until he jumped on home plate with both feet.

Only then did Robinson join his teammates for the long walk across the field to the clubhouse in center. When he reached the Brooklyn locker room, he threw his glove into his locker. A few minutes later, he made his way over to the Giants dressing room, where he quietly offered Durocher his congratulations, their earlier battles forgotten for a moment.

The Robinson winter wasn't a total loss. Rachel was pregnant, and son David was born the following May. His birth led the family from Brooklyn to a larger home in St. Alban's, Queens.

In the spring, the Dodgers-Giants wars resumed yet again. Despite their loss to the Giants in the playoffs, the Dodgers were favored to win the National League pennant in 1952.

The two clubs proved that their late season battle the year before was no fluke. The Dodgers led early, then lost their lead when New York swept Brooklyn in three straight games at the Polo Grounds in late May. But the next day the Giants fabulous young center fielder, Willie Mays, entered the Army. New York could not make up for his loss.

The Dodgers pulled back into first on June 1. Joe Black, Brooklyn's twenty-eight-year-old rookie pitcher, hurled the club into the lead with a 3-2 win over Chicago as the Giants dropped a double-header. Black, picking up the slack as Newcombe was lost to the Army and Branca succumbed to arm miseries, was the fourth African-American on the Dodgers roster, still the most in baseball.

Robinson continued to lead the Dodgers offense. He was elected to the all-star game as the NL's starting second baseman once again, and cracked a first-inning home run off the Yankees Vic Raschi, one of only three National League hits as the AL continued its domination of the mid-season exhibition with a 3-2 win.

Although the Giants hung close the rest of the season, they were never able to catch the Dodgers. On August 25 the Dodgers lead was up to 10 1/2 games, and they clinched the pennant on September 23.

Robinson had, for him, an average season. He hit .308, cracked a career-high 19 home runs, knocked in 75, scored 104 runs and stole 25 bases. At age thirty-three, he was no kid, but he remained one of the most dangerous men in all baseball.

The Yankees found out just how dangerous in the first game of the World Series which started

Robinson is congratulated by Stan Musial as he crosses home plate after hitting his first All-Star Game home run in the first inning of the 1952 game in Philadelphia.

(*Associated Press, National Baseball Library, Cooperstown, N.Y.*)

in Brooklyn on October 1. He led off the second inning of the scoreless game with a home run into the lower left field stands for a 1-0 Brooklyn lead. This set the tone for the game. Snider and Reese also knocked home runs and Joe Black shut down the Yankees on six hits to win 4-3.

Game Two was decided in the sixth inning. With the Yankees leading 2-1, Mantle legged out a bunt single. Woodling singled and Mantle went to third on a wild pitch before Berra walked to load the bases. The next play proved critical.

Joe Collins hit a sharp ground ball right at Robinson. He ceded the run and tagged Berra, then flipped to first for an apparent double play. But Hodges dropped the perfect throw and Mantle scored. Two batters later, Billy Martin

hit a three-run homer to put the game out of reach. Vic Raschi spun a three-hitter and struck out nine Dodgers to win 7-1. At the plate, all Robinson could manage was a walk in four appearances.

The Series moved to the Stadium for Game Three. New York scored first to take a 1-0 lead. In the Dodgers third, Furillo doubled, then Reese beat out a bunt to move him over. Robinson followed with a long fly to Mantle to tie the score 1-1.

Entering the eighth, Brooklyn led, 2-1. Robinson led off with a single to center, then, ever the aggressor, raced to third when Campanella singled to left. He scored on Pafko's sacrifice fly to make the score 3-1.

It was not enough. In the bottom of the inning Berra homered off a tiring Preacher Roe to draw the Yankees to within one.

With one out in the ninth, Reese singled. Jackie then followed with a hit of his own to send the shortstop to second base. Reese and Robinson had combined for fifty-four stolen bases during the regular season, yet relief pitcher Tom Gorman neglected to pay attention to them. They both took off and Reese ended up at third with Robinson at second.

Campanella popped out to Rizzuto at short for the second out. Then Gorman got two quick strikes on Andy Pafko.

His next pitched glanced off Yogi Berra's glove.

Berra spun around, frantically looking for the ball. As it bounced away, Reese raced home.

On second, Robinson broke as soon as he saw the ball roll free and never stopped.

Robinson roared around third as Berra finally tracked down the ball some seventy-five feet away. It was no contest. Between Robinson and Berra, it couldn't be. Jackie scored easily to put the Dodgers up by two.

Allie Reynolds exacted his revenge for the Game One loss in Game Four. Led by Robinson, the Dodgers harangued him all game. "We kept

Robinson toeing the bag at third (left) after his steal in Game Five of the 1952 World Series. A disappointed Gil McDougald covers third too late to make the play.

Robinson's hard-charging running (below) defined the essence of his game.

(both photographs , National Baseball Library, Cooperstown, N.Y.)

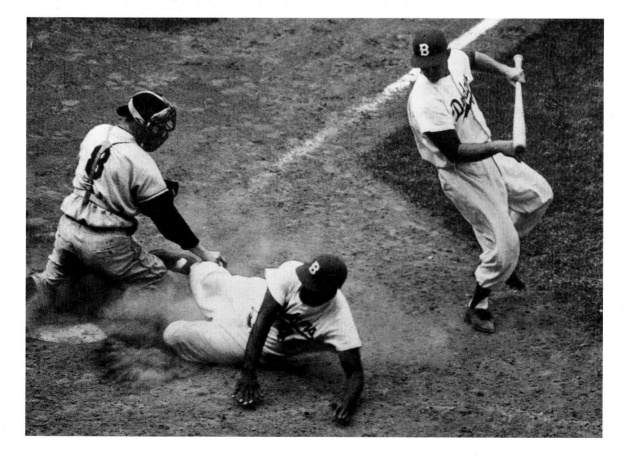

One of the classic mini-rivalries within the framework of the Dodgers-Yankees rivalry was between Robinson and Yankees catcher Yogi Berra. Robinson tormented Berra and the rest of the Yankees with his relentless hellbent baserunning. His steals of home are the stuff of legend. (National Baseball Library, Cooperstown, N.Y.)

Hurler Allie Reynolds (center) beat the Dodgers 2-0 in Game Four of the 1952 World Series to tie the Series at 2-2. To his right is Mickey Mantle, with Johnny Mize to his left.
(Associated Press)

yelling to Reynolds to fire those fastballs and he'd peter out in the fifth inning," he told the press after the game, "He petered out, he did like hell." Reynolds struck out ten, catching Robinson looking three times, and won 2-0.

Jackie got the Dodgers going in the second inning of Game Five. He worked a walk off Ewell Blackwell, and took second when Shuba's grounder to second took a bad hop. Then Robinson made the kind of play that gave his opponents nightmares. Campanella tried to move the runners along with a bunt. He missed the pitch.

The Yankees miscommunicated. McDougald charged and Rizzuto failed to cover third. When Robinson saw the base free, he took it, then scored on Pafko's single.

The Yankees hung on, scoring five in the fifth

to go ahead 5-4 before the Dodgers came back to tie the game and send it into extra innings. But Erskine shut the Yankees down, Snider doubled home Cox in the eleventh, and Carl Furillo deprived Johnny Mize of a home run with a great leaping catch over the wall in right to preserve the win. The Dodgers went up in the Series, three games to two, but that win proved to be the last victory for the Dodgers that season.

The Yankees came from behind to take Game Six, 3-2, then hung on to win the finale, 4-2. Robinson, who'd done a little bit of everything in the first five games, was held to a single hit in the last two. It was "wait till next year" again for the Dodgers.

Next year wasn't like the other years for Jackie Robinson. He showed up at spring training overweight, and at age thirty-four, his body was finally

In March 1953 Dodgers Manager Charlie Dressen named rookie Jim "Junior" Gilliam as his second baseman and moved Robinson to third. (National Baseball Library, Cooperstown, N.Y.)

beginning to betray him. Charley Dressen immediately put him on a diet, but wasn't really bothered by Robinson's condition. It provided an excuse to tinker with the Dodgers lineup. At Montreal in 1952, second baseman Jim "Junior" Gilliam had been the best second baseman in the league since Robinson, hitting .310 and fielding everything. On March 17, Dressen decided to make Gilliam his second baseman and move Robinson to third.

The move wasn't popular. Robinson felt like he was being forced out, plus he wasn't at all comfortable at the hot corner. Third baseman Billy Cox, who many considered to be the best fielder in the league, was bitter and resentful. He felt he was paying the price of placating Robinson. Jackie, however, publicaly toed the company line, saying, "Whatever is good for the

Robinson leaps to spear a liner off the bat of Danny O'Connell of the Pirates at Ebbets Field on September 22, 1953. (Bettmann Archives)

club goes." In private, he told some out-of-town writers that he expected to return to second base.

Dressen was serious. Even though Gilliam didn't hit during camp, he remained at second and at the top of the lineup. The changes took hold and Robinson became less and less diplomatic. Billy Cox was incensed, and when some Dodgers ribbed him about losing his job to a black player, their words touched a nerve. Buzzy Bavasi had to come to camp and calm Cox down, telling him he'd see plenty of playing time as a utility man, filling in at short for Reese and at third when the Dodgers decided to spell Hodges at first and move Robinson across the diamond. For the moment, he was satisfied.

Jackie was slow to come around at the new position. While third requires quickness, and not speed, that was precisely where Robinson was beginning to have trouble. And his arm, never the best, took a while to adjust to the longer throw.

Robinson opened the season at third, batting fourth in the Brooklyn lineup, but Dressen soon made good on his promise. Only Cox did not become the utility man, Robinson did.

When Hodges slumped early, Jackie was moved to first. When he started hitting again, Robinson went back to third. He occasionally filled in at second, and even played one game at shortstop. But Jackie actually spent the bulk of the season in left field.

The result was the most powerful offensive lineup in baseball. Gilliam was the perfect lead-off hitter as he led the league in triples and added 100 walks to his .278 batting average. Hodges, Snider and Campanella all hit more than thirty home runs and knocked in well over 100, Furillo led the league with a .344 average. Reese was his old steady self and Cox hit .291, and Robinson proved he still had it by hitting .329 with 95 RBIs and 17 stolen bases. The

Robinson teaches Jack, Jr. the finer points of the game.
(International Soundphoto)

Dodgers 955 runs were the best in baseball, more than 150 more than the Yankees.

It took awhile for Brooklyn to get all the pieces in place. Despite a 50-31 record at the all-star break, they led Milwaukee by only 1 1/2 games. After the break they won sixteen of nineteen to break the race apart. Brooklyn clinched the pennant on September 12; the earliest clinching date since the NL began playing a 154-game schedule.

For once, the Dodgers began the Series well-rested, their pitching staff strong. And once again, their opponents were the New York Yankees. Carl Erskine, a twenty-game winner in 1953, drew the starting assignment for Game One.

He wasn't ready, struggling with his control in the first and walking two. Bauer and Martin both tripled, Martin's hit going over the head of Robinson in left, and the Yankees led, 4-0. Brooklyn made it a game by scoring five late runs

Dodgers Manager Charley Dressen (left) gives Robinson the Golden Shoe "Athlete of the Year" award. Presenting the award is Sam Abrams of the shoe industry.
(International News

Mickey Mantle of the Yankees hits a grand slam in the 1953 World Series. (*Courtesy of the Boston Herald*)

to tie the score, but Joe Collins' home run put New York ahead to stay, and they won, 9-5.

In Game Two, Preacher Roe held the Yankees to two hits and nursed a 2-1 lead into the seventh. Then Billy Martin turned on a pitch and pulled it high down the left field line.

Robinson raced over, tracked the ball through the shadows, turned awkwardly at the low fence in front of the left field boxes, and reached over his head. He missed the ball. It fell into the stands for a home run and a tie game. Mantle hit a two run homer in the eighth, and New York won again.

Jackie blamed himself for the loss. "I trailed it," he said of Martin's fly. "I should have caught it. When it left the bat I knew the ball was hit pretty good, so I went back, figuring I'd catch it here," he said, gesturing shoulder high. "But it kept carrying. I guess an experienced left fielder would have gone back to the wall right away

instead of trailing the ball. I just didn't play it right."

Brooklyn and Robinson came back in Game Four. Erskine rebounded and pitched magnificently, twirling a no-hitter through four before New York scored a single run in the fifth. Then, as the *Herald Tribune* reported simply, "Robinson awoke."

Dressen thought Jackie was slumping and had dropped him to seventh in the order, the lowest of his career. Jackie responded by taking extra batting practice before the game.

It paid off. With one out in the fifth, he drilled the ball off the screen in right field. Instead of pulling up at first, he kept going, eluding Hank Bauer's throw to second with a hook slide.

Jackie wasn't finished. As Pitcher Vic Raschi worked on Billy Cox, Robinson danced off second, worrying Rizzuto into making a dash for the bag. Raschi started to make a throw, but stopped, his foot still stuck to the rubber. Robinson took third on the balk and scored standing up to tie the score when Cox bunted.

There was more Robinson in the sixth. With Snider on second he smacked a single to left, giving the Dodgers a 2-1 lead. New York came back to tie the game, but Campanella won it with an eighth-inning home run. The Dodgers were still alive.

In Game Four, Jackie continued to show why many considered him the best clutch player in the game. The Dodgers needed to jump out early, and Robinson again came through. In the first inning, he singled home Gilliam to put the Dodgers ahead, and they went on to an easy 7-3 win. Robinson was pulled from the game late for defensive reasons, and his replacement, Don Thompson, snuffed a New York rally by throwing out Billy Martin at home.

The Yankees played like the Yankees in Game Five, crushing four home runs and winning 11-7. The Series now returned to Yankee Stadium, and the Dodgers had to win Game Six to keep their title hopes alive. But this time they solved Erskine. After two innings, New York led 3-0, and the score stayed that way until the sixth.

With one out, Robinson doubled to the wall in the left field corner. Still the best base runner in the game, he caught McDougald napping at third and stole the base uncontested. Campanella rolled to Rizzuto, and Robinson stole a run.

The Dodgers tied the game in the ninth when Snider walked and Furillo homered. But to beat the Yankees, you had to play all nine innings. New York had one more at bat.

That was all they needed. Bauer walked, then Mantle and Martin singled. Ballgame. The Yankees were champions once again.

Soon after the Series Robinson left on his annual barnstorming tour with the Jackie Robinson All-Stars. While much had changed in 1953, what was most important had remained the same. Jackie Robinson's Dodgers were still looking for their first World Championship.

Death of an Unconquerable Man

By Red Smith

In the scene that doesn't fade, the Brooklyn Dodgers are tied with the Phillies in the bottom of the twelfth inning. It is 6:00 p.m. on a late September Sunday, but the gloom in Philadelphia's Shibe Park is only partly due to oncoming evening. The Dodgers, champions-elect in August, have frittered away a lead of 13 1/2 games, and there is bitterness in the dusk of this last day of the 1951 baseball season. Two days ago, the New York Giants drew even with Brooklyn in the pennant race. Two hours ago, the numbers went up on the scoreboard: New York 3, Boston 2. The pennant belongs to the Giants unless the Dodgers can snatch it back.

With two out and the bases full of Phillies, Eddie Waitkus smashes a low, malevolent drive toward center field. The ball is a blur passing second base, difficult to follow in the half light, impossible

to catch. Jackie Robinson catches it. He flings himself headlong at right angles to the flight of the ball, for an instant his body is suspended in midair, then somehow the outstretched glove intercepts the ball inches off the ground.

He falls heavily, the crash drives an elbow into his side, he collapses. But the Phillies are out, the score is still tied.

Now it is the fourteenth inning. It is too dark to play baseball, but the rules forbid turning on lights for a game begun at two o'clock. Pee Wee Reese pops up. So does Duke Snider. Robin Roberts throws a ball and a strike to Robinson. Jackie hits the next pitch upstairs in left field for the run that sets up baseball's most memorable playoff.

Of all the pictures left upon memory, the one that will always flash back first shows him stretched at full length in the insubstantial twilight, the unconquerable doing the impossible.

The word for Jackie Robinson

is unconquerable. In *The Boys of Summer*, Roger Kahn sums it up: "In two seasons, 1962 and 1965, Maury Wills stole more bases than Robinson did in all of a ten-year career. Ted Williams' lifetime batting average, .344, is two points higher than Robinson's best for any season. Robinson never hit 20 home runs in a year, never batted in 125 runs. Stan Musial consistently scored more often. Having said those things, one has not said much because troops of people who were there believe that in his prime Jackie Robinson was a better ball player than any of the others."

The point is, he would not be defeated. Not by the other team and not by life.

Another picture comes back. Robinson has taken a lead off first base and he crouches, facing the pitcher, feet fairly wide apart, knees bent, hands held well out from his sides to help him balance, teetering on the balls of his feet. Would he be running? His average was 20 stolen bases a year, and the columnist Bugs Baer wrote that "John McGraw demanded more than that from the baseball writers."

Yet he was the only base runner of his time who could bring a game to a stop just by getting on base. When he walked to first, all other action ceased. For Robinson, television introduced the split screen so the viewer at home as well as the fan in the park could watch both the runner on first and the pitcher standing irresolute, wishing he didn't have to throw.

Jackie Robinson established the black man's right to play second base. He fought for the black man's right to a place in the white community, and he never lost sight of that goal. After he left baseball, almost everything he did was directed toward that goal. He was involved in foundation of the Freedom National Bank.

He tried to get an insurance company started with black capital, and when he died he was head of a construction company building housing for blacks. Years ago a friend, talking of the needs of blacks, said, "Good schooling comes first."

"No," Jackie said, "housing is the first thing. Unless he's got a home he wants to come back to, it doesn't matter what kind of school he goes to."

There was anger in him, and when he was a young man he tended to raise his falsetto voice. "But my demands were modest enough," he said, and he spoke the truth. The very last demand he made publicly was delivered in the mildest of terms during the 1972 World Series. There was a ceremony in Cincinnati saluting him for his work in drug addiction, and in his response he mentioned a wish that he could look down to third base and see a

black manager on the coaching line.

Seeing him in Cincinnati recalled the Dylan Thomas line that Roger Kahn borrowed for a title: "I see the Boys of Summer in their ruin." At fifty-three Jackie was sick of body, white of hair. He had survived one heart attack, he had diabetes and high blood pressure and he was going blind as a result of retinal bleeding in spite of efforts to cauterize the ruptured blood vessels with laser beams. With him were his wife, Rachel, their son, David, and daughter, Sharon. Everybody was remembering Jack Jr., an addict who beat the heroin habit and died at twenty-four in an auto accident.

"I've lost the sight in one eye," Jackie had told Kahn a day or so earlier, "but they think they can save the other. I've got nothing to complain about."

Unconquerable is the word.

Walter "Red" Smith was the most widely syndicated and highly respected sports columnist of his day. His literate essays appeared in The New York Herald Tribune, Women's Wear Daily *and* The New York Times. *He was awarded the Pulitzer Prize in 1976. The native of Green Bay Wisconsin and graduate of Notre Dame died in 1982.*

RUNNING IT OUT: 1954-1956

At the end of the 1953 season Jackie Robinson completed a six-year run as the greatest player in the game. Beginning in 1948, his second season with the Dodgers, Robinson's annual average was .323, with 108 runs scored, 33 doubles, 7 triples, 15 home runs, 91 RBIs, 99 walks and 13 stolen bases. Only Stan Musial and Ted Williams could match his numbers over the same time period, but neither was close to him defensively or on the base paths, and neither could match his versatility. Most remarkably, Robinson performed at this high level after getting the latest start by a star offensive player in the history of the game. No one, *ever*, has come close to matching his offensive production, with such little experience while beginning a career so late in life.

Another measure of Robinson's talent is to look at those who hit around him in the Brooklyn lineup. For most of those years, the Dodgers lineup included three other Hall of Famers—Reese, Snider and Campanella—and another man, Hodges, who may well deserve to join them in the Hall. Yet even on a team of stars, Robinson was the undisputed offensive leader, the player opponents and teammates alike looked toward to start the Dodgers attack and keep it going. For most of these six seasons, Robinson hit cleanup for the Dodgers, the spot usually reserved for a team's undisputed run producer.

Robinson was just that, but he was even more dangerous on base than he was in the batter's box. While he stole relatively few bases when compared to some contemporary players, no one in the game was better at stealing third or home, and no one approached his ability to use the steal to upset the opposition. A pitcher could give up a hit to Robinson and rationalize that he had made

Whether turning a double play of running the bases, all eyes were on Jackie when he was on the field.
(both photographs, Bettmann Archives)

a bad pitch. But when Robinson stole a base, or danced provocatively off the bag, or took an extra base that no other player in the league would have thought about taking, it was a direct affront to the opposition. With one mad dash he could simultaneously upset the pitcher, catcher and one or two fielders.

It wasn't so much the bases he stole that caused the problem for the opposition; it was the bases he threatened to take. Pitching with Robinson on base was akin to trying to defuse a bomb while under gunpoint. There was no margin for error.

For it was on the bases that Robinson could, from the very beginning, fight back. There, he could be the intimidator, more effective than any fastball thrown at his own head. That combination of arrogance and aggressiveness was the key to his eventual acceptance by his fellow players and the public.

Fans, even those who hated him for his color, loved watching him on base. Even on television, he appeared kinetically charged, the one living being on a field of somnambulists. His own teammates knew instinctively what he meant for their chances to win. The opposition learned that cheap shots at Robinson always came at a price. He would find a way—his way, some day, some time—to retaliate. The only thing worse than having Robinson on base was having an embarrassed or angry Robinson on base. The Phillies and Cardinals paid the price for their indiscretions during his rookie season for the rest of his career. Robinson played in-your-face, cutthroat baseball, the likes of which had not been played since the time of Cobb and has not been played since. The baseball field was the battleground on which he waged his joyous, righteous war for equality.

Robinson's unique style of play has been credited to what he learned in the Negro Leagues, but there is more to it than that. Of all the players who eventually came to the major leagues from Negro baseball, none matched Robinson on the basepaths, not even those with more speed and more baseball talent. For Robinson was not so much a product of athleticism as he was of will, and his own refusal to fail. When he entered organized baseball, he lacked experience but had athletic talent to burn. He used his speed and gridiron aggressiveness to make up the difference. As he gained experience, his combined talents almost made it seem as if he wasn't playing fairly. Yet even as his skills eroded, he could still make plays of which no on else in baseball dared to dream.

By the time Robinson arrived at spring training in 1954, he had increasing trouble keeping off weight, and at age thirty-five, his reflexes were beginning to erode. Jackie was changing, and so were the Dodgers. Only a couple of weeks after the World Series, Charley Dressen pressed for a two or a three-year contract. After all, he rea-

Though remembered mostly as a second baseman, Jackie ventured into the outfield on occasion. (Bettmann Archives)

The Dodgers celebrate Manager Charley Dressen's 55th birthday on September 20, 1953 at Ebbets Field. Taking part in the celebration are (l-r): PeeWee Reese, Bob Millikin, Billy Cox, Charlie Dressen and Jackie Robinson.
(Courtesy of The Boston Herald)

Robinson says goodnight to his children at their St. Albans, Long Island home. They are David (22 months), Sharon (4 years) and Jackie Jr. (7 years).
(Transcendental Graphics)

soned, in three seasons he had led Brooklyn to two pennants and missed a third by a single pitch.

O'Malley refused. The Dodgers only gave out one year contracts, so Dressen left and O'Malley replaced him with Walter Alston, an organization man. With Alston at the helm, O'Malley had someone who would do what he wanted, something he hadn't been able to count on with Dressen.

The Dodgers were stunned by the move. They were a veteran club, and had little respect for the minor league manager. Alston sensed this, and got off on the wrong foot with many of the Dodgers veterans, including Robinson. It also didn't help that the Dodgers were getting older. Reese, Robinson, Hodges, Campanella and Furillo, the heart of the club, were all over thirty.

They had grown accustomed to doing things a certain way, and didn't like being told differently.

Robinson started the season in left, but after only six games was put back at third, leading Red Smith to write at the beginning of the season, "Well kids, here we go again." Alston benched Cox, who was hitting only .180, and put Sandy Amoros in left, where Robinson had struggled. Jackie's .400 batting average kept him in the line-up.

He continued his hot hitting, but was soon in and out of the lineup with heel trouble. The Dodgers played patty-cake with first place through the month of May, then slipped back when Campanella was injured and the Giants went 24-4 in June and to take control. Leading the way for New York was center fielder Willie Mays, who, in the midst of his first great season, was considered by most to be the best player in baseball.

Robinson was growing frustrated. By early June he was hitting .340, but his inability to stay in the lineup bothered him.

In the fourth inning of a game against Milwaukee on June 2, the Dodgers went wild with umpire Lee Ballanfant when he lost track of the count to Johnny Logan of the Braves. Robinson came running in all the way from left field to add his two cents. Logan walked and Eddie Mathews then cracked a grand slam home run.

In the top of the fifth, Robinson was in the on-deck circle and started in on Ballanfant again. "Get in there and hit," warned the umpire, "or I'll throw you out of the game." Jackie, stalling for time in a light rain, snapped back something like, "Go ahead, you've already messed up the game enough already." Robinson's wife might claim she'd never heard him curse, but no ballplayer could say the same.

Ballanfant tossed him. As Robinson approached the dugout, he flipped his bat toward

In the fourth inning of a game against the Milwaukee Braves on June 2, 1954, Robinson accidently lost the grip of his bat as he flung it towards the Dodgers dugout following his ejection following an argument with umpire Lee Ballanfant. The bat struck a female fan in the head, prompting Robinson to apologize. (Courtesy of The Boston Herald)

the dugout. It slipped from his hand and struck a female fan in the head.

Robinson apologized, but the press was all over him, using the incident to vent some long held grudges. The Dodgers tried to stay close to the Giants as they surged, but when New York swept Brooklyn at the end of June, the writing was on the wall. The Dodgers hung close for the rest of the season, but didn't have the pitching to catch the Giants.

Jackie was hobbled much of the second half and his average slumped to .311. He played in only 124 games and was often pulled late for defensive reasons. All his numbers were down, as he stole only seven bases and scored only 62 runs. He wasn't a number four hitter anymore.

Robinson, at age 33, was already beginning to slow down slightly as the fatigue shows in this photo taken after the Dodgers defeat in the seventh game of the 1952 World Series. This series was Robinson's fourth, and each time the Dodgers lost to the Yankees. (Associated Press, National Baseball Library, Cooperstown, N.Y.)

In the 1954 Series between the Yankees and Indians, Willie Mays made one of the great catches in the history of the game off of this Vic Wertz drive to center. While Jackie's career was coming to a close, Willie was establishing himself as one of the top play-ers in the game. (Associated Press)

Despite Robinson's heroics, Dodgers Owner Walter O'Malley once called him "Rickey's prima donna." Today, family differences are forgotten as O'Malley's son Peter serves on the Board of The Jackie Robinson Foundation.
(National Baseball Library, Cooperstown, N.Y.)

When Robinson arrived at spring training the following season, he soon found out he wasn't even a regular anymore. His relationship with Alston, never more than cordial, deteriorated. As the club played its way north, Alston indicated that several positions were still up for grabs, including third base, where Robinson had spent most of the spring. "I haven't made up my mind whether it will be Robinson or Don Hoak," Alston told the *Herald Tribune's* Roger Kahn. He then added, "an ailing Robinson won't help us," in reference to a sore arm that had bothered Jackie on and off all spring.

Robinson responded in the press that his arm was fine. As for Alston, Robinson said, "I can't talk to him. I don't know why, but I just can't." Privately, he felt that as far as Alston and the

O'Malley's were concerned, he wasn't "their kind of Negro," self-deprecating and cheerful, like Campanella.

Alston fumed at Robinson's breach of protocol. He was tired of defending himself to sports writers, who openly wondered why he was fooling around with Gil Hodges and Junior Gilliam in the outfield and Reese at second base. "He [Robinson] ought to talk to me before he talks with the damn press," Alston said. Then the manager refused to say whether or not Jackie would be in the lineup on opening day, saying, "I'm not going to say. It wouldn't do any good telling the damn press." Alston and Robinson met, and according to Robinson, "He told me to stop stirring things up," which included his self-references as a Dodgers "irregular."

When the season opened in Brooklyn on April 13, Robinson was playing third and hitting sixth in the Dodgers lineup that included Reese, Hodges and Gilliam at their usual spots. Jackie was rejuvenated. After an earlier double, he came to bat in the seventh with Reese on third and Snider on first.

Robinson dropped a vintage bunt. It rolled past pitcher Max Surkont and the Pirates had no play as Reese scored and Snider and Robinson were safe at second and first. The Dodgers went on to win, 6-1.

The Dodgers opened the season with ten straight wins before the Giants beat them 5-4 on April 22. The game marked the annual resumption of the Dodgers-Giants wars, which were getting uglier each year. For each club, winning was no longer enough. There were two games going on, one reflected by the final score and another by more discrete events.

Robinson started the hidden season in the seventh. He stabbed Davey Williams' line drive, and after making the catch, happily flipped the ball back into the air in a "Take that" gesture to the Giants bench. In the on deck circle, Alvin Dark

Robinson is greeted by his Dodgers teammates at the Polo Grounds after hitting a home run against the defending World Champions on May 29, 1955. (Courtesy of The Boston Herald)

slammed his bat to the ground as he glared at Robinson, and Durocher mocked Robinson by throwing his cap into the air.

The war escalated two days later. Sal "The Barber" Maglie—his nickname richly deserved because of his uncanny ability to give batters a close shave—started for the Giants. In the fourth inning, with the score tied 1-1, Maglie sent a pitch under Roy Campanella's chin.

Campy then struck out, bringing Robinson to the plate. Jackie upped the ante.

He pushed a bunt down the first base line, intending to make first baseman Whitey Lockman field the ball so Maglie had to cover first. Once he did, Robinson intended to send him into right field.

Jackie's bunt was perfect, and Maglie started over to cover first. But he'd been through this with Robinson before. He sensed what was about to happen and stopped. Giant second baseman Davey Williams raced to first and turned to take the throw.

Jackie hit him like he was going through the line at UCLA, kneeing Williams hard in the lower back. Williams held the ball for the out, but went sprawling to the ground. Al Dark raced over from shortstop and tried to throw a punch at Robinson, but umpire Tom Gorman interceded.

Williams was shaken up, but stayed in the game. One inning later, Dark sought revenge.

He doubled and, sensing a chance to get even, rounded second and headed for third. Robinson took the throw well ahead of Dark's arrival. As Dark barreled in, spikes high, Robinson stepped to the side and slammed the ball into the second baseman's face, losing his grip. Dark was safe, and for a time, the two clubs called a cease-fire.

The Dodgers won, 3-1, and after the game

Before the 1954 All-Star Game, Roy Campanella and Yogi Berra enjoy a light moment at Cleveland Municipal Stadium.
(Associated Press)

Robinson denied hitting Williams intentionally, although he said everything with a nod and a wink. His teammates made a show of coming up to him and thanking him for providing protection. Later, Jackie admitted that while he did slam Williams, he hadn't noticed it was Williams—not Maglie—on the base until it was too late.

The incident, which set the tone for the season, is not without its tragic aspect. Williams was hurt worse than he realized on the play. The collision injured his spine and eventually knocked him from the lineup by mid-season. He never played again.

Robinson was surprisingly unapologetic about the affair. He saw his response as the expected outcome of Maglie's challenge, and besides, players had been banging into him for years, truly trying to hurt him. He hadn't meant to hurt Williams. It was just an unfortunate accident.

The Dodgers, united as much by their dislike of Alston as anything else, went on to to win another eleven in a row to effectively wrap up the pennant by the middle of May. Robinson stopped hitting and Alston benched him in favor of Hoak, but Hoak couldn't keep the job. For the remainder of the season the two men split the position.

Meanwhile, the Dodgers made good on their fast start and ran away with the pennant, going wire-to-wire and finishing 13 1/2 games ahead of second place Milwaukee. Newcombe went 20-5, Snider cracked 42 home runs and knocked in 136 to lead the club. Robinson played in only 105 games, hitting .256, knocking in only 36 runs, and stealing twelve bases.

It was October in the 1950s, and that meant that the Dodgers and the Yankees squared off once more in the World Series. At first it appeared as if it would end like all the others had, with a world championship in the Bronx.

Don Newcombe reads his reviews in the Daily News. (Associated Press)

Yogi Berra and Whitey Ford of the Yankees were always tough on the Dodgers. (The Boston Herald)

The first game of the 1955 World Series was marked by controversy as Robinson scores on an eighth inning steal of home. Robinson was called safe by umpire Bill Summers after stealing home on Hall of Famers Whitey Ford and Yogi Berra. (Bettmann Archives)

The first game was played in Yankee Stadium on September 28 with Whitey Ford matched against Newcombe.

In the second inning, Furillo homered. Then Robinson, as he had done so many other times in his first at bat in a Series game, came through. He hit a long triple to left center and scored on Don Zimmer's single to give Brooklyn a 2-0 lead.

New York immediately tied the score as Newcombe again failed to match his regular season performance in the post season. The Dodgers scored once more in the third, but the Yankees tied, then went up 4-3 on Joe Collins' home run. He homered again in the sixth to put the Yankees up 6-3.

Brooklyn threatened in the eighth. Furillo singled, and with one out, Robinson hit a ground ball off McDougald's knee at third for a two-base error. Zimmer flew to left center, scoring Furillo, and Robinson, still a great baserunner, alertly went to third.

Frank Kellert pinch-hit for the pitcher. Ford, in full windup, threw a ball.

On third, Robinson watched closely. Ford took his time winding up, and hardly gave Robinson a glance between pitches. Robinson weighed his options. Trailing by two runs, baseball's proverbial "book" said not to take chances. But as Robinson later wrote "I suddenly decided to shake things up . . . I just took off and did it. I really didn't care whether I made it or not—I was just tired of waiting." Four World Series losses to New York in nine seasons were enough. As soon as Ford stepped back to begin his windup, Robinson broke from third and bore down on Yogi Berra.

All at once, Robinson wasn't the aging, overweight veteran, but the fleet aggressive athlete of his youth. A shocked Berra grabbed the pitch and dove toward him as Robinson aimed his slide at the front of the plate.

The two met in a small cloud of dust. Plate

Yankees catcher Yogi Berra reacts to Jackie Robinson's steal of home in the eighth inning of Game One in the 1955 World Series.

umpire Bill Summers jumped from behind the plate and flung both arms in the air. Robinson was safe.

Berra scrambled to his feet already screaming and threw a tantrum. Even today, Berra still believes Robinson was out.

No matter. Jackie's mad dash cut New York's lead to one, 6-5, yet the Dodgers failed to capitalize on the play and New York hung on to win.

The next day, the Dodgers slipped farther back. Tommy Byrne went the distance and even drove in two runs in the four-run New York fourth. Brooklyn managed only five hits and two runs, one scored by Robinson after a fifth-inning walk. The Yankees led the Series two games to none.

Back at Ebbets Field, Brooklyn thundered back. Johnny Podres went the distance, Campanella homered, and the Dodgers roared to an 8-3 win. Robinson contributed two hits and proved once again that he wasn't quite finished. In the eighth, he doubled down the left-field line. Elston Howard fielded the ball, and saw Robinson, apparently asleep, take a big, lazy turn. He gunned the ball to second.

In other seasons the Yankees scouting report probably would have warned Howard what to expect, but Robinson hadn't done much running in 1955. The play was a favorite old trick. The idea was to goad the left fielder into throwing behind him, then run like hell for third. Howard did his part, and so did Robinson.

Now Brooklyn had the momentum. They shook off a 3-1 third-inning deficit to take the lead on home runs by Campanella and Hodges, then went ahead for good on a three-run shot by Snider in the fifth to win 8-5. Robinson went hitless.

The Dodgers won for the third time in a row in Game Five. Rookie Roger Craig went six strong innings and Snider gave him all the help he needed by stroking two home runs and a dou-ble. Robinson knocked in an insurance run in the eighth with a single, and Brooklyn won, 5-3.

With New York reeling, all of Brooklyn stood poised to celebrate when Game Six began back in the Bronx. But in the first, Brooklyn starter Karl Spooner struggled with his control and the Yankees scored five runs. Ford scattered four hits, and New York knotted the Series at three-all with a 5-1 win.

The seventh game of the 1955 World Series was the biggest game in Brooklyn Dodgers history. Pitcher Johnny Podres succeeded where so many Brooklyn hurlers had failed in the past, scattering eight hits and shutting out the Yankees. Hodges knocked in Campanella in the fourth, then added a sacrifice fly in the sixth to give the Dodgers the only two runs they needed. In the ninth, Sandy Amoros made a fine over-the-shoulder running catch of Berra's drive, then doubled MacDougald off base to save the game. Brooklyn won, 2-0, to capture the Series.

Ironically, in this most important game, Jackie Robinson, for nearly a decade the soul of the Dodgers, did not appear. His earlier escapades on the base paths had proved costly. When he rose on the morning of October 4, his left heel throbbed. He had hurt it in Game Five trying to beat out a double play. Don Hoak played in his stead while Robinson watched from the bench.

Still, all Brooklyn celebrated. They had waited a long, long time to do so. The Dodgers, at last, were champions of the world.

The Jackie Robinson who reported to training camp in 1956 barely resembled the player who first donned a Dodgers uniform in 1947. Robinson's close-cropped hair was peppered with gray, his face was round and full, his legs had turned heavy and his once-trim body no longer looked lean.

He was beginning to feel the effects of diabetes and often complained that he felt exhausted. He learned he had the disease sometime during the

Robinson was one of a small but solid core of longtime Dodgers who savored the 1955 World Championship triumph over the Yankees. (National Baseball Library, Cooperstown, N.Y.)

Pee Wee Reese played beside Jackie for much of his career. Here, Reese is speechless after receiving presents on his 36th birthday.
(International News Photo)

season, a factor which contributed to his eventual decision to retire.

He wasn't the only Dodgers player who looked past his prime. The team that had played together for much of a decade had aged. Yet the Dodgers were determined to prove their world championship performance was no swan song. They wanted to win again.

The Dodgers weren't certain where Robinson fit into their plans in 1956. He didn't move well enough to play the outfield much anymore, and they weren't sure he'd stay healthy enough to play third. In the off-season they acquired Cub third baseman Ransom Jackson for some insurance.

Jackie surprised everyone and beat out Jackson for the starting spot in spring training. On opening day he again manned third and hit sixth in the order.

The Dodgers raised their world championship banner before the start of the game on April 17, but the Phillies ruined the celebration with an 8-4 win. Brooklyn's age showed and the club got off to a slow start, playing barely .500 baseball over the first two months, giving hope to Milwaukee, Cincinnati, St. Louis and Pittsburgh, all of which spent time at or near the top of the standings while the Dodgers wallowed in third or fourth.

On May 15, in a shocking move, the Dodgers purchased Sal Maglie from the Cleveland Indians, who had acquired him the previous season from the Giants. Maglie, a certified Dodgers killer if there ever was one, was surprised when he joined the club and found Jackie Robinson the first to greet him.

Robinson wasn't just being magnanimous. For all their battles, he admired Maglie's toughness,

Yogi Berra and Roy Campanella. AL and NL MVP's in 1955.

knew he could help the Dodgers win, and was happy he wouldn't have to hit against him anymore.

The Dodgers started playing better in midseason, but Jackie struggled. He was in and out of the lineup with a series of nagging injuries and just wasn't hitting. While he had thought long and hard about his life after baseball, he now made more specific plans.

Any other star of Robinson's magnitude would have looked to baseball for future employment, but under the O'Malley regime Robinson knew that was not just unlikely, it was unwanted. Acceptance on the field had been earned grudgingly, day-by-day. Baseball wasn't ready to welcome him into the fold of the front office or

coaching ranks. Besides, he had built a large home in Stamford, Connecticut, and didn't want to leave metropolitan New York. Robinson started sending out feelers into the private sector.

Entering September, the Braves held a two-game lead. As the pennant race heated up, Robinson started showing signs of life. He underwent an interesting transition. Just as, in the beginning of his career, he used his aggressiveness and speed to mask his shortcomings in other areas, now he used aggressiveness and guile to mask his loss of skills. The effect was the same.

On September 1, the Dodgers swept the Giants. Robinson keyed a ninth-inning rally in the first game with a single and two stolen bases, his fourth and fifth of the series. Alston had moved him back into the cleanup spot, and he was starting to turn back the clock.

On September 12 the Braves came into Brooklyn leading by one game. Maglie was magnificent as he held the Braves in check. In the eighth inning of the biggest game of the year, with Brooklyn clinging to a 2-1 lead, Robinson proved he was not quite finished.

Jackie singled and moved to second. As pitcher Ernie Johnson of the Braves got set, Robinson feinted a dash to third, worrying the pitcher into trying a pick off attempt.

The throw sailed into right center. Robinson tore around the bases and made it home with the insurance run. A visibly upset Johnson then gave up a home run to Hodges and the Dodgers held on to win, 4-2, to move into first.

The Braves won the next day to regain the lead, but the Dodgers pulled back in front on September 15 when Robinson backed Newcombe's 3-0 shutout of the Cubs with a two-run, third-inning double.

For the next ten days the Braves and Dodgers traded first place back and forth by percentage points almost every day. On September 25, Maglie hurled a no-hitter over the Phillies and Robinson again keyed the Dodger attack with his baserunning.

In the second, he led off with a double and Gil Hodges walked. This time Robinson lured pitcher Russ Meyer into a pickoff try. His throw sailed into center, allowing both runners to advance and taking away the double play. Robinson then scored on a ground ball and Campanella hit a two-run homer. Brooklyn won, 5-0.

They finally moved into first place for good on September 29. Brooklyn swept two from Pittsburgh while the Braves lost a twelve-inning heartbreaker to St. Louis.

In the second game of the double-header, a 3-1

win, Robinson again played a key role. With the Dodgers nursing a 1-0 lead, Jackie beat out an infield hit. Amoros was awarded first on catchers' interference, and then Hodges brought both men home with a triple.

The next day, the final day of the season, the Dodgers won the pennant. Amoros and Snider each cracked two home runs and Robinson contributed a solo shot in the Dodgers 8-5 defeat of Pittsburgh. Milwaukee finished one game back.

They faced the Yankees once more in the Series. Maglie got the call to pitch Game One in Brooklyn. Robinson remained at third base, remained fourth in the batting order, and remained the leader of the Dodgers attack.

In the first, Mantle hit a two-run home run to put New York ahead. Then Robinson got into the act. One more time he got the Dodgers on the board in a World Series game, homering off

Whether on the diamond, on the court or on the course, Jackie was always one of the best athletes.
(Associated Press)

Robinson slides home against the Wes Westrum of the Giants at the Polo Grounds in 1956. (Associated Press)

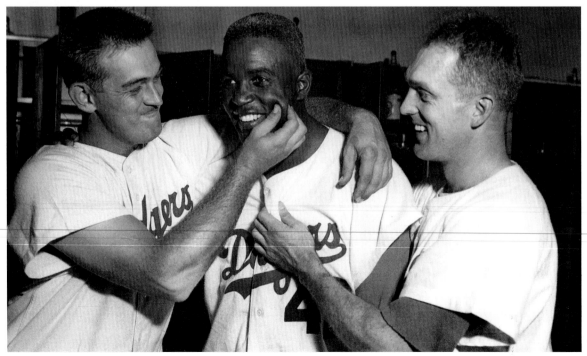

Winning Dodgers pitcher Clem Labine pinches Robinson in delight as starting pitcher Carl Erskine looks on. Robinson drove in all three runs in a 3-2 victory over the league-leading Braves on August 1, 1956. (Transcendental Graphics)

of Ford into short left to lead off the inning. Hodges singled and Furillo doubled to plate a second run and the game was tied. They broke it open in the third when Hodges hit a three-run shot and went on to win, 6-3.

Game Two was a slugfest. The Yankees jumped out to a 6-0 lead before Brooklyn roared back with six second-inning runs. They scored again in the third to go up one, but New York tied the score in the top of the fourth.

In the bottom of the inning Snider singled then Robinson came through again with a base hit of his own. Hodges doubled both men home and Brooklyn rolled to a 13-8 win.

At the Stadium for Game Three, Robinson again got Brooklyn on the board early. It was classic Jackie. He led off the second inning with a walk, moved up a base on Hodges' bleeder, took third on a fly ball, and scored on Campanella's sacrifice. It wasn't enough, however, as the Yankees used Slaughter's three-run homer to collect a 5-3 win.

They tied the Series in Game Four behind Tom Sturdivant's six-hitter, 6-2. Robinson contributed a walk and ninth-inning double, scoring Brooklyn's final run, but again, it wasn't enough.

Game Five was legendary. Don Larsen pitched a perfect game to beat Maglie and his five-hitter, 2-0. Yet of all the Dodgers that day, it was Robinson who came closest to solving the Yankee pitcher. In the second inning he hit a wicked line drive off Andy Carey's glove at third. A younger Robinson would have beaten it out, but the ball caromed straight to McDougald who threw him out by a step. In the fifth, Jackie turned on a pitch and drove it foul to deep left, then flew out to Bauer just in front of the warning track. Then in the eighth, he hit a sinking liner to the left of Carey at third, who reached out and caught the ball at his knees.

Returning to Ebbets Field for Game Six, the Dodgers regrouped. Reliever Clem Labine, in only his fourth start all season, shut the Yankees down on seven hits and kept them scoreless. His counterpart, Yankees pitcher Bob Turley, was even better. Through nine he gave up only three hits.

But Turley had to go ten. With one out, Gilliam drew a walk. Reese sacrificed and New York walked Snider intentionally to get to Robinson. The move made sense. After all, the left-handed Snider was the most dangerous hitter in the league in 1956. It made more sense for Turley, a righthander, to face Robinson.

The Dodgers clubhouse was full of reporters anticipating the end of the game when Robinson stepped in the box. They huddled around Ralph Branca, who, although not eligible for the Series,

Mickey Mantle (Courtesy of the Boston Herald)

*Jackie and Rachel share
a quiet moment with
their children.*
(Courtesy of the Boston Herald)

was serving as Brooklyn's batting practice pitcher. Branca echoed the feeling of Dodgers fans everywhere as he stared at the television and pleaded, "Come on Jackie, come on Jackie."

Robinson swung at Turley's first pitch and just missed it, fouling the ball back into the stands along third base. Then Turley threw a low fast ball. Jackie reached down and pulled the ball to left. Yankee outfielder Enos Slaughter, fooled a bit by Robinson's swing, broke awkwardly then ran straight to his left.

The Brooklyn crowd held its breath. The ball stayed in the air but appeared catchable. Then it carried. Slaughter misjudged how hard the ball was hit. It was over his head.

Slaughter jumped, but came down with nothing but the promise of Game Seven. The ball hit the base of the concrete wall, then ricocheted back past him so quickly he had no chance to catch the rebound. Gilliam scored, and the Dodgers won, 1-0.

One last time, the Dodgers season came down to a final game against the Yankees. Like so many others before, it ended in defeat.

New York jumped out to an early lead as they pounded Newcombe, but no Dodgers pitcher could stop the Yankees that day. They slammed four home runs and won going away, 9-0, to win the Series.

Robinson went hitless in his final major league appearance. In the first, he grounded into a double play. In the fourth, he tried to bunt for a hit, but got the ball in the air and pitcher Johnny Kucks made a fine running catch at the third base line. In the seventh he walked, but was doubled off, his aggressiveness working against him for once, when Hodges lined to McDougald at short.

Jackie Robinson came to bat for the last time in a Dodgers uniform in Ebbets Field in the borough of Brooklyn, New York, with two outs in the ninth inning. Kucks, summoning the last of his strength, struck him out.

In less than a year after Robinson's departure from the Dodgers, the team itself would desert Brooklyn and head west to Los Angeles. Robinson is shown bidding farewell to Ebbets Field in February 1957. (Courtesy of The Boston Herald)

Yet Berra dropped the ball, as if the game that at first didn't let Robinson in, couldn't let him go. Another player in a similar situation, trailing by nine runs in the last game of the World Series, may have simply stood there and allowed the catcher to tag him.

Jackie Robinson had never played that way. He didn't now.

He dropped his bat and lit out for first, running hard down the line, just as he had when he entered the league, not running away from anything, but for something. Berra calmly tossed the ball to Moose Skowron, and Robinson was out.

He ran hard until he passed the bag, then pulled up, turned and jogged back toward the Brooklyn dugout. The Yankees celebrated.

Consequently, Brooklyn soon mourned.

For ten years Jackie Robinson thrilled baseball fans as he helped lead the Dodgers to six pennants and one World Series title. He is shown leaving the clubhouse at Ebbets Field for the last time in February 1957.

(Bettmann Archives)

Jackie Robinson: Hope by Example

By Ira Berkow

November, 1972

Days after Jackie Robinson's death, I was still thinking of a lunch I had with him about four years ago. I had walked into his midtown Manhattan office, where he was vice-president of Chock Full O'Nuts, to pick him up. He was on the phone, legs up on his desk, talking to some friend about a celebrity golf event to which, this year, he had not been invited. Robinson had gone to several previous tournaments in the series.

He wanted the friend to find out why there was no invitation. Did it have anything to do with some of his recent controversial remarks about "racism in America." "We'll give it a good fight," Robinson said, smiling. He had the shaft of his glasses in his teeth.

Jackie Robinson, it seemed to me, enjoyed the fight. Even then, at age 49, suffering from diabetes, failing eyesight that would render him virtually blind before his death, high blood pressure, heart trouble, and the drug addiction of his son, Jackie Jr., he was still combative.

"Look at Jackie now," wrinkled Satchel Paige told me a couple years ago, "and his hair's white and you'd think he was my grandfather."

He didn't sound old, though speaking in that dynamic falsetto he sounded more like Liberace than you'd expect of this rough ex-ballplayer, who was so menacing on the bases, who suffered so many pitchers trying to stuff baseballs in his ear, who broke the color barrier in a white elitist game and had to live with "black bastard" echoing through the dugouts and the caverns of his mind.

At Jackie's funeral, however, the Rev. Jesse Jackson's eulogy rang through the great vaulted Riverside Church, and the phrase for Jackie Robinson had changed from "black bastard" to "black knight."

Robinson had become a Hall of Famer, but his place in history does not stop at Cooperstown. Baseball provided the setting for a milestone in the American human rights struggle. Robinson helped open the doors of opportunity not only in sports but also in many other areas of America.

Jesse Jackson compared Robinson to Louis Pasteur and Gandhi and Martin Luther King and Jesus, as a man who gave others hope by example. This may seem a wild exaggeration. But if you were a 13-year-old black boy like Ed Charles living in Florida—where blacks were still lynched—it was not so wild.

" I owe so much to Jackie Robinson," said Charles, an ex-major-league infielder. "All black players do. We tend to forget. I never will. When Jackie Robinson came through my home town with the Dodgers in 1947, it was the biggest day of my life. It was the biggest day of all our lives.

"I realized then I could play in the major leagues. They pushed the old people to the ballpark in wheelchairs and some came on crutches and a few blind people were led to the park.

"When it was over, we chased the Dodger train as far as we could with Robinson waving to us from the back. We ran until we couldn't hear the sound any more. We were exhausted but we were never so happy."

I told Robinson at lunch that day that I had recently been in Chicago and had talked casually with a black shoeshine boy in his early teens. I asked who his favorite baseball player was.

"Ernie Banks," the bootblack said. "Willie Mays, too. Yeah, I wanna be a ball player too. Like him."

I asked the fellow if he wanted to be a ball player like Jackie Robinson, too?

"Who?" he asked. "Never heard of him."

This was neither sad nor surprising to Robinson. He dealt in realities.

"It's true that many black kids have never heard of me," he said. "But they haven't heard of the Montgomery bus boycott in 1956, either. And that was the beginning of Dr. King's nonviolent movement. They don't get any kind of black history in their school books. They want it. They read only about white society. They're made to feel like nonpersons. This is frustrating. It's up to the power structure of this country to understand these kids. Then the burnings, the muggings, the dope, the despair, much of what plagues this country will be greatly lessened.

"Black athletes playing today

carry prestige. They can be very significant in explaining the problems and encouraging the kids. But I've been out of baseball for 12 years. The kids look at me like I'm just an old-timer."

The "old-timer" fought until he died. He fought for better housing, he fought for better schooling, he fought for greater say for blacks in government, he fought for a black manager in baseball.

While he angered the mossbacks who thought he wanted too much too fast, he continued to inspire others with the courage of his fight that would encompass freedom for all men.

"No grave can hold his body down," said Jesse Jackson, "it belongs to the ages. His spirit is perpetual. And we are all better because a man with a mission passed our way."

Ira Berkow is an award winning sports columnist for *The New York Times*. His books include a biography of sportswriter Red Smith and a collection of essays entitled *Pitchers Get Lonely Too*.

THE BURDEN OF HISTORY 1957-1972

After the season, Robinson rested at his home in Stamford. He was exhausted, and was having trouble adjusting to living with diabetes. According to some reports, he even went into a diabetic coma and was briefly hospitalized. Jackie had given everything he had to baseball, to Rickey's grand experiment, to the Dodgers, and to those to whom he meant so much, African-Americans. He soon learned that he was not through, but had simply changed games.

Jackie knew he was finished with baseball, but before making any announcement he first wanted to secure a job. He met with a man named Bill Black, who owned the "Chock Full O'Nuts" chain of coffee shops. Most of Black's employees were African-American, and he wanted Robinson to serve as vice president of personnel. While Robinson was negotiating with Black, he turned his focus toward the actual retirement. He wasn't sure how to handle it.

He felt he owed O'Malley nothing, so he worked out a deal to break the story in *Look* magazine for $25,000. In early December, he met with Black and agreed to sign on with the company for a salary of $50,000 over two years. He planned to call Dodgers General Manager Buzzy Bavasi and let him know he was contemplating retirement, but under the terms of his contract with *Look* he couldn't actually say he was retiring until the story appeared in print.

Bavasi beat Robinson to the punch and called

When the Dodgers announced they had traded Robinson to the Giants on December 13, 1956, the future Hall of Famer had already negotiated a contract to work for Chock Full O'Nuts. Nonetheless, he posed for this news photo in the wake of the trade.
(Courtesy of The Boston Herald)

him, requesting a meeting. Robinson was ironing out the details of his contract with Chock Full O'Nuts, and told Bavasi it would be a day or two before he would be free. When Jackie called back on December 13, Bavasi shocked Robinson into silence. The Dodgers had traded him to the Giants for $30,000 and relief pitcher Dick Littlefield, a journeyman with a career record of 27-44. Jackie wanted to tell Bavasi he was through, but could not. Then he contacted the Giants, and without explanation, tried to get them to hold off announcing the deal. They refused.

When the story of the trade broke, Brooklyn rose in anger. O'Malley, already unpopular, became a pariah, as picketers marched on Ebbets Field. Trading Robinson was as unthinkable in Brooklyn as tearing down Ebbets Field, an idea O'Malley had already floated with disastrous results.

Robinson escaped to California with his family to avoid the press until the story appeared in *Look*. When it did, Jackie found himself at the center of a controversy.

The article contained few surprises, and is best summed up by Robinson's admission that "my legs are gone and I know it." Some members of the press, already upset that he had chosen to break the story in a magazine piece, took him to task for putting a price on his retirement and stringing the Dodgers and Giants along, intimating that he was selfish and primarily interested in the money.

And the fact was that New York still wanted him. The Giants had slipped all the way to sixth place in 1956, and despite the presence of Willie Mays, drew only 629,000 fans, the second worst total in baseball. New York President Horace Stoneham believed Robinson would help out at the gate, and offered him a blank check to play one more season.

Robinson was tempted. The money was not

insignificant. But in the end, Robinson decided to remain retired. Some had written that the entire retirement story was simply a ruse Robinson had designed to extract more money from the Giants. It wasn't, but the only way Jackie could prove it was to stay retired. So he did. The trade was rescinded by mutual agreement.

Unlike other star players, Robinson's departure from baseball was marked by no teary press conference. Robinson simply stayed away from the game.

Baseball had changed dramatically in the ten seasons that had passed since he first played for the Dodgers. By the 1957 season, more than fifty other African-Americans had followed Robinson from the Negro Leagues to the majors. Over a hundred were active in the minor leagues. While some teams, like the Boston Red Sox, had yet to sign a black player, it was apparent that no team in baseball could hope to compete successfully without African-Americans.

Yet Major League Baseball had missed a golden opportunity. The slow pace with which most clubs became integrated made them miss out on some of the best post-war Negro League talent. When the pace picked up in the mid-1950s, the talent pool had shrunk.

The Negro Leagues were dead. Efforts to bring all-black baseball under the wing of the National Association as some kind of minor league failed. The Negro National League folded after the 1950 season, while the Negro American League limped on until 1955. Attendance was almost nonexistent. The major leagues were beginning to sign young talent right off the sandlot fields instead of scouting the Negro League for players, and a new generation

Robinson displays the letter dated January 14, 1957, drafted on Chock Full O'Nuts letterhead, announcing his retirement from baseball.
(Courtesy of The Boston Herald)

Robinson greets Chock Full O'Nuts workers on his first day as vice president of personnel on March 5, 1957. (Transcendental Graphics)

of players found the constant barnstorming tiresome.

Only a few teams remained, and most of those did not last the decade. The few that did were forced to add "clowning" to their repertoire, serving as baseball's version of the Harlem Globetrotters.

At the same time, baseball began to abandon the inner city. Major league teams did little to encourage black fans to come to the ballpark. Television showed blacks participating in other sports, and baseball's role in the black community began to erode. Young black men and children turned to other games, primarily basketball. When Robinson signed in 1946, organized baseball, had it moved aggressively, could have had

the black community for the asking. But by the time Robinson retired, baseball had sent the black community another message, suggesting that despite the abundance of black stars, they were not really welcome in the game after all. When Robinson left baseball, so too did many black fans.

Robinson tried to settle into the businessman's life. He took his job seriously, taking an active role in all matters concerning Chock Full O'Nuts employees. But Robinson's real job remained what it had been since he joined the Dodgers organization in 1946. He was a warrior in the fight for racial equality.

He lent his name and time to a number of organizations. Unfettered by baseball, he was

Together with the Rev. Martin Luther King, Robinson received an honorary doctorate of law at commencement exercises at Howard University in 1957.

(Associated Press)

now able to take a more active role. Within a few years he became a member of the board of directors of the NAACP, hosted a weekly radio show that discussed racial matters, and authored a column in the *New York Post* ghost-written by Alfred Duckett. Although the column appeared in the sports pages, it almost always concerned the cause of civil rights.

The tenor of that debate was changing. Emerging black leaders found Robinson's generally cautious approach increasingly anachronistic. Yet Robinson was still one of the most visible black men in America, one whom whites found far less threatening than figures like Martin Luther King. Robinson didn't realize it, but his public role was in transition. Jackie Robinson was no longer at the center of the struggle, as he had been with the Dodgers, but rather a symbol in the quest for equality.

In 1960 Robinson took leave from Chock and worked on Hubert Humphrey's presidential campaign. When Kennedy defeated Humphrey, Robinson met with the president-to-be and was put off.

He threw his support to Richard Nixon, whom he had known for several years and who had courted his support. The move proved costly.

The *Post* canceled his column, but more significantly, Robinson's backing of Nixon later marked him as a man out of touch with the times. The Democratic Party eventually won the support of black voters and took up the cause of civil rights.

Baseball did not entirely forget Robinson. In 1962, in his first year of eligibility, he was elected to the Hall of Fame. Yet even that great honor was not without controversy. Bob Feller was voted to be inducted that same year, and told reporters that he would have preferred to have entered the Hall with Roy Campanella, whom he considered to be the better choice.

Robinson steered clear of any controversy. Accompanied by his family and Branch Rickey,

Robinson was inducted on July 23, 1962, before a crowd of 5,000.

In this earlier era, the induction ceremonies were far briefer than they are today. The entire ceremony, including remarks by dignitaries and speeches from the inductees, who in addition to Robinson and Feller included Edd Roush and Bill McKechnie, took only thirty-eight minutes.

Robinson gave a short speech, honoring those who meant most to him. "I feel quite inadequate to this honor," he told the crowd. "It is something that could never have happened without three people—Branch Rickey, who was as a father to me, my wife and my mother. They are all here today, making the honor complete. And I don't think I will ever come down from cloud nine."

The inscription on the plaque reads:

Jack Roosevelt Robinson
Brooklyn N.L. 1947-1956

Leading N.L. batter in 1949. Holds

fielding mark for second baseman

playing 150 or more games with .992.

Led N. L. in stolen bases in 1947 and

1949. Most Valuable Player in 1949.

Lifetime batting average .311. Joint

record holder for most double plays

by second baseman, 137 in 1951.

~~Led second baseman in double~~

plays 1949-50-51-52.

It is probably the most inadequate plaque honoring a player in the Hall, as it fails to mention Robinson's pioneer status in the game and reduces his career to a few since-broken fielding marks. Indeed, any child who reads the plaque

Jackie talks on the phone after learning of his election to the Baseball Hall of Fame.

Jackie and Rachel pose with Ricky in this 1962 photo. (Associated Press)

Robinson is shown with Bob Feller following their playing careers. In the autumn of 1946 they led barnstorming teams that played each other on the west coast. (Courtesy of The Boston Herald)

On July 23, 1962 Robinson received his greatest honor as he was inducted into the National Baseball Hall of Fame. Strangely, his plaque makes no mention of his achievement as the first African-American to play in the majors in the 20th century. (UPI, National Baseball Library, Cooperstown, N.Y.)

Jackie and Floyd Patterson (left) met with Mrs. A.D. King after her home was bombed in 1963. The bombing triggered riots in Birmingham, Alabama.

and learns of Robinson for the first time must wonder why he is even in the Hall. If any of the plaques call out to be replaced, Robinson's does. One more appropriate might read:

Jack Roosevelt Robinson
Kansas City Monarchs 1946
Brooklyn N. L. 1947-1956

First African-American to play in the major
leagues in the 20th century.
Greatest baserunner of his time.
Led Dodgers to six World Series.
National League Rookie of the Year in 1947.
Most Valuable Player and N.L.
batting champion in 1949.
Lifetime batting average .311

After the Nixon campaign, Robinson returned to his work with Chock Full O'Nuts, then struck

up another political alliance, this time with Liberal Republican New York Governor Nelson Rockefeller. In January of 1964 he had a falling out with William Black and resigned from Chock. He signed on with the Rockefeller presidential campaign, but when Rockefeller lost, Robinson was briefly out of work. He tried and failed to start an insurance company and served as Chairman of the Board for Freedom National Bank before joining Rockefeller's administration as a special assistant for community affairs.

Increasingly, Jackie was coming under attack from other black leaders, who now viewed him as something of a sell out. He kept coming out on the wrong side of issues and had a difficult time retaining his political influence outside Rockefeller's office. Robinson began to fade as a national figure.

At the same time, there was trouble at home. His son, Jackie Jr., was drafted and sent to

Robinson visited Harlem with Vice President Hubert H. Humphrey in 1968.

With New York Gov. Nelson Rockefeller to his right, Robinson speaks to members of the National Newspaper Publishers Association in 1968. Jackie supported Rockefeller's run for the White House. (UPI)

Vietnam. Jackie Jr. had never been comfortable with his father's celebrity status, and in his younger years he had trouble in school and had gotten into minor trouble with the law. When he returned from Vietnam in 1967, like so many others, he had a drug problem. After drifting for a year, he was finally arrested in March of 1968. Robinson was embarrassed, but stuck by his son, although he began to reassess his own parenting. "I guess I had more of an effect on other people's kids than I had on my own," wondered Jackie. He placed Jackie Jr. in rehab, and his son was able to overcome his addiction.

Robinson broke with Rockefeller over the Governor's support of Nixon in 1968. By now, Jackie was questioning whether the Republican party had much to offer the black community.

He took a position with a fledgling restaurant chain, "Sea Host," but the chain went bankrupt. He then began work on his autobiography, *I Never Had It Made* with writer Alfred Duckett.

Jackie and Rachel were financially secure. She had long since moved from nursing into academia, and Robinson, despite some failed investments, was far from broke. Son David and daughter Sharon were both doing well, but Robinson's health was slowly deteriorating. He was reportedly less than conscientious about his diet and medication, and began to have trouble walking and seeing. He had gained weight through lack of activity and his hair was almost white. He sometimes used a cane.

Some observers have commented that Robinson grew old fast, a condition they credit

Jackie met with President Nixon prior to the All-Star Game in 1969. Commissioner Bowie Kuhn is looking on in the background.

to the immense pressure he faced during his playing career. Such statements are absurd. Diabetes is a serious debilitating disease, one that kills thousands of Americans each year. And while it is true that many diseases are exacerbated by stress—and Robinson certainly had his share—to blame his physical condition solely on stress is to ignore reality and demean those with the disease.

On June 16, 1971, Jackie Junior died in a car accident on the Merritt Parkway in Connecticut. His son's death had a severe impact on Jackie.

His health deteriorated for the next year to the point where he could barely walk and was nearly blind. Doctors even wanted to amputate his leg. He made his last national appearance on October 15, 1972, in a television interview just prior to the second game of the World Series between the Oakland A's and the Reds in Cincinnati. Although his health was failing, Jackie still had goals. He told the interviewer that while he was pleased to be at the World Series, "I will be more pleased the day I can look over at third base and see a black man as manager." It was his last controversy, as some took him to a task for interjecting politics into the World Series.

Nine days later, on the morning of October 24, 1972, Robinson collapsed at home. He was pronounced dead of a heart attack on his way to the hospital.

Jackie Robinson's enduring legacy extends beyond the events of that single day in April of 1947 when he made his first appearance in a Major League Baseball game. That day belonged to Branch Rickey.

All the remaining years were Robinson's. For Jackie, it was not enough simply to get his foot in the door. He broke the door down and went on, crashing through each and every barrier he found, always pressing forward and moving ahead, testing the dimensions of who he was and who America would allow him to be.

Robinson did not choose his life; he was chosen. Another man may not have allowed himself to be embraced by Branch Rickey's paternal hand. Robinson accepted it, yet remained wholly his own man. Another man may have broken under the weight of that responsibility. Jackie Robinson grew stronger. Another man may have acted in regard only to himself. Jackie Robinson accepted the challenge and carried others along with him. Another man may have confined his efforts to the baseball field. Jackie Robinson extended his fight from the national pastime to the national character.

Baseball's color line didn't just break and disappear. Robinson ground it into dust with his relentless play and indomitable spirit. He even extended his crusade. He knew that if his efforts were to end on the baseball field, he, and the rest of us, would be the ultimate losers. Another may have seen retirement as an opportunity to recede from view. Jackie Robinson used retirement to enlarge the playing field, to continue to give himself to a larger battle.

Even death did not stop him. Robinson's fight continues today. Each time he is remembered his memory reminds us of the trials that still lie ahead. One victory does not make a season, one season a career, or one lifetime the legacy of a man. The cause goes on. There are games still left to play.

Twenty-five hundred people attended his funeral at Riverside Church on October 27. In

In March, 1968, Robinson accompanied Jackie Jr. following his arraignment in Circuit Court in Stamford, Connecticut for narcotics possession and a weapons violation. (Transcendental Graphics)

In his last public appearance on October 15, 1972, only nine days before his death, Robinson threw out the first pitch at Game Two of the World Series at Riverfront Stadium. He would comment in a television interview before the game that while he was happy to be at the series, "I will be more pleased when I can look over at third base and see a black man as manager."

(Courtesy of The Boston Herald)

Jackie's casket is carried from Riverside Church in New York on October 27, 1972. Pallbearers included basketball great Bill Russell as well as former teammates Don Newcombe and Ralph Branca.

(AP)

the crowd were celebrities from the worlds of sports, entertainment, politics and civil rights. The Reverend Jesse Jackson delivered the eulogy.

As he dramatically recounted Robinson's life, Jackson's speech transfused the proceedings with something approaching joy.

At the conclusion of the eulogy, Jackson noted that on Robinson's tombstone it would read "1919 dash 1972." There, said Jackson, "On that dash, is where we live. And for everyone there is a dash of possibility, to choose the high road or the low road, to make things better or worse."

"On that dash," continued Jackson, his voice rising to a crescendo, "he snapped the barbed wire of prejudice." Then, in call and response with the crowd, Jackson spoke in transcendent metaphor.

"His feet danced on the base paths!"

"But it was more than a game."

"Jackie began playing a chess game."

"He was the black knight."

"In his last dash, Jackie stole home and Jackie is safe."

"His enemies can rest assured of that!"

"Call me nigger, call me black boy! I don't care!"

The crowd called out and roared, more like a crowd at baseball game as they cheered one last time for what Robinson did and for who he was, for how he played the game, the way he lived his life, and the world, so much improved, that he left behind.

ROBINSON BY THE NUMBERS

More so than many other members of baseball's Hall Of Fame, the playing career of Jackie Robinson is not quantifiable. During his peak, when most ballplayers usually perform best, Robinson was not even playing. And when he did play, much of what he did best—harass pitchers, take the extra base, cause bad throws—could not be measured. Still, Robinson's raw numbers do bring out a few interesting observations.

First, what if Robinson had been able to play in his prime? What if, for instance, Robinson had been able to play professional baseball immediately upon leaving Pasadena Junior College and had been able to enter the major leagues in 1941? Because of his ankle injury, he may have been declared 4-F and been able to play during the war years. What record might he have put together?

There is, of course, no "correct" answer to these questions, just as there is no "correct" answer to speculation about Ted Williams' record had he not missed three seasons due to military service. That need not stop us from trying to provide an answer. From 1948 through 1953, Robinson's peak, his average season consisted of 537 at bats, 108 runs, 174 hits, 23 doubles, 7 triples, 15 home runs, 92 RBIs, 23 stolen bases and a .323 batting average. It is not outlandish to think that Robinson, playing against sub-par competition during the war, may well have been able to meet those marks in his six "lost" seasons. Were that the case, his career totals might well have looked something like this:

G	AB	R	H	2B	3B	HR	RBI	SB	AVG.
2267	8104	1595	2562	412	95	229	1282	334	.316

That would place Robinson in the top fifty or seventy-five players of all time in most of these offensive categories, and until the last decade or so, identify him as one of only a handful of players to possess both power and base stealing ability.

In the past two decades "sabermetrics," a group of statistics that go beyond those listed above have been created and promoted, by the members of the Society for American Baseball Research. The reference book *Total Baseball*, includes many of these such statistics. Suffice to say that had Robinson been able to play an additional six seasons at anything close to the level I have suggested above, according to sabermetric's "total player rating," (a stat which tries to assess players cumulative value, taking into account the differences in eras), Robinson would have about sixty points, about 18th all-time, just behind guys like Mel Ott and Lou Gehrig and just ahead of Joe Morgan and Jimmie Foxx.

One other statistic stands out when one looks at Robinson's career. In his ten seasons with the Dodgers, they finished in first place six times. In the other four seasons, they finished second three times—by a total of only eight games—and third once, by seven and a half games. Moreover, in these ten seasons and six subsequent

World Series appearances, Robinson played regularly at four different positions—first base, second base, third base, and outfield, primarily left field. Only Pete Rose has performed as widely, and Robinson, in most estimations, was the far better fielder.

The following statistics were culled from the standard sources and supplemented by the authors' research.

JACKIE ROBINSON
SEASONAL STATISTICS

Note: **Bold** denotes led league, underline denotes led team, when known.

NEGRO LEAGUE BATTING
KANSAS CITY MONARCHS, NEGRO AMERICAN LEAGUE

YR	G	AB	R	H	2b	3b	HR	RBI	K	BB	AVG	OBP	SLG	SB	CS
1945	47	163	36	63	14	4	5	23	na	na	.387	na	na	13	na

MINOR LEAGUE BATTING
MONTREAL ROYALS, INTERNATIONAL LEAGUE

YR	G	AB	R	H	2b	3b	HR	RBI	K	BB	AVG	OBP	SLG	SB	CS
1946	124	444	**113**	<u>155</u>	25	8	3	66	27	92	**.349**	**.461**	.464	40	15

MAJOR LEAGUE BATTING
BROOKLYN DODGERS, NATIONAL LEAGUE

YR	G	AB	R	H	2b	3b	HR	RBI	K	BB	AVG	OBP	SLG	SB	CS
1947	151	590	<u>125</u>	<u>175</u>	<u>31</u>	5	<u>12</u>	48	36	74	.297	.383	.427	**29**	na
1948	147	574	<u>108</u>	<u>170</u>	<u>38</u>	8	12	<u>85</u>	37	57	.296	.367	.453	22	na
1949	156	593	122	<u>203</u>	<u>38</u>	<u>12</u>	16	<u>124</u>	27	86	**.342**	.432	**.528**	**37**	na
1950	144	518	99	170	<u>39</u>	4	14	81	24	80	.328	.423	.500	12	na
1951	153	548	106	185	<u>33</u>	7	19	88	27	79	.338	.429	.527	<u>25</u>	8
1952	149	510	<u>104</u>	157	17	3	19	75	40	106	.308	**.440**	.465	24	7
1953	136	484	109	159	34	7	12	95	30	74	.329	.425	.502	17	4
1954	124	386	62	120	22	4	15	59	20	63	.311	.417	.505	7	3
1955	105	317	51	81	6	2	8	36	18	61	.256	.381	.363	12	3
1956	117	357	61	98	15	2	10	43	32	60	.275	.383	.412	12	5
TOT.	1382	4877	947	1518	273	54	137	734	291	740	.311	.410	.474	197	30

WORLD SERIES BATTING

Note: **Bold** denotes series leader.

YR	G	AB	R	H	2b	3b	HR	RBI	K	BB	AVG	OBP	SLG	SB	CS
1947	7	27	3	7	2	0	0	3	5	4	.259	.323	.333	**2**	0
1949	5	16	2	3	1	0	0	2	2	**4**	.188	.350	.250	0	0
1952	7	23	4	4	0	0	1	2	5	**7**	.174	.366	.304	**2**	0
1953	6	25	3	8	2	0	0	2	0	1	.320	.360	.400	**1**	0
1955	6	22	5	4	1	1	0	1	1	2	.182	.250	.318	**1**	0
1956	7	24	5	6	1	0	1	2	2	5	.250	.379	.416	0	0
TOT.	38	137	22	32	7	1	2	12	15	23	.234	.344	.358	6	0

MINOR LEAGUE FIELDING

YR	Pos	PO	A	E	PCT.
1946	2B	261	385	10	**.985**

MAJOR LEAGUE FIELDING

YR	Pos	PO	A	E	PCT.
1947	1B	1323	92	16	.989
1948	2B-116				
	1B-30				
	3B-6	514	342	15	**.983**
1949	2B	395	421	16	.981
1950	2B	359	390	11	**.986**
1951	2B	**390**	**435**	7	**.992**
1952	2B	353	400	20	.974
1953	OF-76				
	3B-44				
	2B-9				
	1B-6				
	SS-1	238	126	6	.984

YEAR	POS				
1954	OF-64				
	3B-50				
	2B-4	166	109	7	.975
1955	3B-84				
	OF-10				
	2B-1				
	1B-1	100	183	10	.966
1956	3B-72				
	2B-22				
	1B-9				
	OF-2	169	230	9	.978
TOTAL		4007	2728	117	.983

DODGERS RECORD– THE ROBINSON YEARS 1947-1956

YEAR	W	L	Pos	Pct.
1947	94	60	1 by 5	.610
1948	84	70	3 by 7.5	.545
1949	97	57	1 by 1	.630
1950	89	65	2 by 2	.578
1951*	97	60	2 by 1	.618
1952	96	57	1 by 4.5	.627
1953	105	49	1 by 13	.682
1954	92	62	2 by 5	.597
1955	98	55	1 by 13.5	.641
1956	93	61	1 by 1	.604
TOT.	945	596		.631
Avg.	94	60		

*includes three-game playoff with New York

SELECTED BIBLIOGRAPHY

As indicated in the introduction, newspapers were the primary source used in the creation of this book. Indeed, it would be impossible to create a book of this kind without utilizing period newspapers. The author urges anyone interested in Robinson to go directly to these sources first. Monographs most useful in the preparation of this volume are listed below, although all sources used are not listed and the author cannot vouch for their accuracy, particularly those editions that are ghost-written. Articles listed include those consulted which do not appear in Myron Smith's *Baseball Bibliography*. More recent offerings are easily accessible through the proliferation of database services now available for both newspapers and magazines.

Three web sites were useful for this project. The Brooklyn Dodgers home page @ www.bayou.com~brooklyn/ contained a wealth of information. Younger readers might enjoy the Jackie Robinson home page @ www.afroam.org/history/Robinson. Additional periodical articles can be found at www.skypoint.com/pub/members/a/ashbury/sabr/sabr_biblio_Jackie_Robinson.

NEWSPAPERS

Game reports for the bulk of Robinson's career were gleaned from the *New York Herald Tribune*, 1946 through 1957, the *New York Times*, 1946 through 1957, and *The Sporting News*. Coverage of Robinson's Negro League and minor league career was obtained from the *Pittsburgh Courier* 1945 through 1948, the *Louisville Courier Journal* 1946, and the *Montreal Gazette*. Information on Robinson's collegiate career was located in the *Los Angeles Times* 1937 through 1941 and the *Los Angeles Sentinel*. Other newspapers consulted include the *Boston Chronicle*, the *Daily Worker*, the *Chicago Defender*, and the *New York Age*.

BOOKS

Allen, Maury. *Jackie Robinson*. New York: Franklin Watts, 1987.

Bruce, Janet. *The Kansas City Monarchs*. Lawrence, Kansas: University Press of Kansas, 1985.

Chandler, Happy and Trimble, Vance. *Heroes, Plain Folks and Skunks*. Chicago: Bonus Books, 1989.

Clark, Dick and Lester, Larry, editors. *The Negro Leagues Book*, Cleveland: The Society for American Baseball Research, 1994.

Cohen, Stanley. *Dodgers!* New York: Carol Publishing Group, 1990.

Durocher, Leo and Linn, Ed. *Nice Guys Finish Last*. New York: Simon and Schuster, 1975.

Eskenazi, Gerald. *The Lip*. New York: William Morrow, 1993.

Falkner, David. *Great Time Coming*. New York: Simon and Schuster, 1995.

Frommer, Harvey. *Rickey and Robinson*. New York: MacMillan, 1982.

Golenbock, Peter. *Bums: An Oral History of the Brooklyn Dodgers*. New York: G.P. Putnam, 1984.

Golenbock, Peter. *Fenway: An Unexpurgated History of the Boston Red Sox*. New York: G.P. Putnam, 1992.

Halberstam, David. *The Summer of '49*. New York: William Morrow, 1989.

Kahn, Roger. *The Boys of Summer*. New York: Harper and Row, 1973.

Kahn, Roger. *The Era*. New York: Ticknor and Fields, 1993.

Kountze, Mabrey "Doc". *50 Sports Years Along Memory Lane*. Medford, Massachusetts: Mystic Valley Press, 1979.

Peterson, Robert. *Only the Ball was White*. New York: Oxford University Press, 1970.

Poiner, Murray. *Branch Rickey: A Biography*. New York: Atheneum, 982.

Robinson, Jackie and Duckett, Alfred. *I Never Had It Made*. New York: G.P. Putnam, 1972.

Robinson, Jackie and Smith, Wendell. *My Own Story*. New York: Greenberg, 1948.

Robinson, Jackie and Rowan, Carl. *Wait 'Til Next Year*. New York: Random House, 1960.

Rogosin, Donn. *Invisible Men*. New York: Atheneum, 1983.

Rosenfeld, Harvey. *The Great Chase*. Jefferson, North Carolina: McFarland, 1992.

Stout, Glenn. *DiMaggio: An Illustrated Life*. Edited by Dick Johnson. New York: Walker, 1995.

Tiemann, Robert. *Dodger Classics*. St. Louis: Baseball Histories, 1983

Tygiel, Jules. *Baseball's Great Experiment*. New York: Oxford University Press, 1983.

Veeck, Bill and Linn, Ed. *Veeck as in Wreck*. New York: Simon and Schuster, 1962.

ARTICLES

Davis, David. "Straight, No Chaser," LA Weekly, August 11-17, 1995.

Kelley, Vic. Memorandum dated 10/25/45 ASUCLA News Bureau.

Libman, Gary, "Jackie Robinson: Recalling a Legend," Los Angeles Times, April 6, 1987.

Nielsen, Ray. "Harold 'Pee Wee' Reese on 'The Jackie Robinson Story'," Classic Images, January 1996.

"Remembering Jackie," special section, USA Today Baseball Weekly, October 25-31, 1995.

Stout, Glenn. "Diamonds Aren't Forever," Boston Magazine, September 1986.

Stout, Glenn. "Off Track," Boston Magazine, September 1988.

Washburn, Pat. "New York Newspaper Coverage of Jackie Robinson in his first Major League Game," unpublished doctoral dissertation, Indiana University, 1980.

Williams, Juan. "Jackie Robinson Fought for Justice in Baseball," Los Angeles Times, May 3, 1987.

Index